Reynolda

A HISTORY OF
AN AMERICAN COUNTRY HOUSE

John F. Blair, Publisher   Winston-Salem, North Carolina

Reynolda
A HISTORY OF
AN AMERICAN COUNTRY HOUSE

by Barbara Mayer

DESIGN BY DEBRA LONG HAMPTON
COVER DESIGN BY LIZA LANGRALL
PRINTED AND BOUND BY R. R. DONNELLEY & SONS

Library of Congress Cataloging-in-Publication Data

Mayer, Barbara, 1938–
Reynolda : a history of an American country house / by Barbara Mayer.
p.   cm.
Includes index.
ISBN 0-89587-155-6 (alk. paper)
1. Historic buildings—North Carolina—Winston-Salem.   2. Winston-Salem (N.C.)—
Buildings, structures, etc.   3. Reynolda House—History.   4. Reynolds family.
I. Title.
F264.W8M39   1997   97–233
975.6'67—dc21

CONTENTS

FOREWORD

In this readable narrative, Barbara Mayer sweeps us through the life passages of an early-twentieth-century Southern country house, the core of a large farming estate. She brings to life the people who built it and cared for it as it passed from one generation to another. She also traces its hairsbreadth escape from irreparable alteration and demolition and, finally, the process by which it was safeguarded for the future through its transformation into a museum of American art.

Since that time, over a million visitors have been drawn to Reynolda House for its art collection, begun in 1967, as well as for its historical and cultural significance. Its board of directors is dedicated to the preservation, exhibition, and interpretation of the collection of American art in the setting of a historic house. The presentation of cultural and educational programs that broaden knowledge and appreciation of American art, literature, and music is also an important part of its mission.

Despite Reynolda House's thirty-year public role, widespread interest in it as a historic site has surfaced only recently with national attention on the American country house. A growing number of scholarly publications have provided a context in which Reynolda now can be understood as belonging to this turn-of-the-century movement. Against this background, the board of directors decided that it was time to tell the story of Reynolda and approved the commissioning of an accurate and informative history. This publication also celebrates the eightieth anniversary of the house.

This project relied heavily on the Reynolda House archive, established in 1993, which centralizes historical documents related to the estate and the Reynolds family. These documents—including letters, postcards, diaries, notes, household inventories, bills, estimates, and blueprints—now constitute a database. Hundreds of vintage photographs, many reproduced in this book, provide an abundant visual chronicle of the house, gardens, grounds, and family. Also enriching the narrative are primary oral histories that preserve the reminiscences of family members and others, many no longer alive, who recalled the early years of Reynolda.

It has been a colossal job to make sense of so much material, and Barbara Mayer has worked diligently to link these spotty but vastly interesting records into a coherent story. It is my sincere hope that this book will help visitors understand the people and events that led to the building and dispersion of the estate, and that it will provide a deeper appreciation of its centerpiece, Reynolda House.

Barbara Babcock Millhouse
President
Reynolda House
  Museum of American Art

ACKNOWLEDGMENTS

In researching and writing Reynolda's story, I asked many questions and received considerable help, which it is a pleasure to acknowledge.

Barbara Millhouse has an encyclopedic knowledge of the history of Reynolda, which she shared generously. Landscape designer Sherold D. Hollingsworth has studied Reynolda's history over many years and readily answered all my questions and supplied additional information. I also made use of her master's thesis, "Prototype for a Landscape Conservation Plan for Reynolda" (North Carolina State University, 1986).

Virtually every staff member with whom I came in contact at Reynolda House extended a helping hand and expressed enthusiastic interest in the progress of the book. I especially thank Nicholas B. Bragg, executive director, and Richard Murdoch, archivist, for their considerable time and effort on this project. Collections manager Ellen M. Kutcher, associate director for development Elizabeth Morgan, librarian and costume curator Ruth B. Mullen, assistant director for programs Marjorie J. Northup, and business manager Heather Gould Smith also gave special assistance.

Margaret Supplee Smith, professor of art

history at Wake Forest University, shared her research, writings, and knowledge of Charles Barton Keen, early-twentieth-century architectural history, Katharine Reynolds, and Reynolda.

John R. Woodard, director, and Julia Bradford, assistant, at the North Carolina Baptist Historical Collection in the Z. Smith Reynolds Library at Wake Forest offered friendly, efficient retrieval of needed files.

Among others who provided enlightenment or helped in some other way were Charles Babcock, Jr., Jane Burton, Sandra Daniels, William Erwin, Alex Glover, Mac Griswold, Dr. Duncan Heron, Dale Jaeger, Teri Jefferson, Ricky Johnson, William and Sandria Kerr, Earline King, the late Joe King, Ed Lash, Lu Leake, Katharine Babcock Mountcastle, Derek Ostergard, Sara Pilling, Bynum Shaw, and Zachary Smith.

Thanks also to Susan Allport, who read a portion of the manuscript to good effect. I mention with special gratitude Gordon Mayer, to whom I wish to dedicate this text. He read the manuscript at several stages and offered many helpful editing suggestions.

INTRODUCTION

Reynolda House is one of a small number of early-twentieth-century American country houses still standing in almost their original form. While its current use as an art museum is different from its earlier function as a home, the house looks much as it did when completed in 1917. The gardens, too, are a reasonable approximation of the ones created eighty years ago.

A visit to present-day Reynolda gives an inkling of its past but does not convey the workings of the place in its full glory in the teens and early twenties. Reynolda—whose feminine ending indicates the central role of Katharine Reynolds in its creation—transcended its role as a family home. Katharine Reynolds and her husband, tobacco tycoon R. J. Reynolds, conceived of their country place about three miles west of downtown Winston, North Carolina, not merely as an imposing residence with attendant pleasure gardens and recreational facilities but as a beacon of light in agriculture and community life.

R. J. Reynolds died only seven months after moving into the house. But thanks to Katharine's influence, the estate was more a self-sufficient community than a mere country house and pleasure ground.

Richard Joshua Reynolds (1850–1918) in 1905

REYNOLDA HOUSE ARCHIVES
Photograph by Eug. Pirou, 23 Rue Royale, Paris

Katharine Smith Reynolds (1880–1924) in 1905

REYNOLDA HOUSE ARCHIVES
Photograph by Eug. Pirou, 23 Rue Royale, Paris

Of course, there *was* a luxurious sixty-four-room house, lavishly equipped and furnished as the centerpiece of the estate. A man-made lake, miles of winding roads, vineyards, greenhouses, formal gardens, a golf course, two tennis courts, and a swimming pool were there for the pleasure of the family and its guests. But these accounted for only a portion of Reynolda's life.

Reynolda had its own post office, two churches, two schools, more than twenty houses for workers, and its own telephone, water, and electric-generating systems. Most of these buildings were designed by the architect of the main house, Charles Barton Keen. The farm and dairy incorporated the latest agricultural knowledge and equipment and were much-admired showplaces.

Katharine Reynolds interacted almost daily with employees and their families, most of whom lived on the 1,067-acre estate, either in Reynolda Village or in the farmworkers' village known as Five Row. These people participated in a complex community life of their own—fishing in the lake, swimming, playing baseball, going to school, attending church, and visiting with one another—which is remembered by survivors and descendants with pleasure.

While unusual in its communal aspects, Reynolda was part of a national phenomenon. In the first three decades of the twentieth century, hundreds of wealthy Americans all over the United States built imposing country places for themselves. Many included splendid gardens, recreational facilities to rival those of a country club, showplace farms that did not need to turn a profit, bodies of water, and more.

Despite the similarities among these properties, each was a singular place, custom-made to a patron's vision, and each that remains tells a unique, personal story. To visit one of them— Reynolda; or Biltmore, George Vanderbilt's place in Asheville, North Carolina; or Kykuit, John D. Rockefeller's home in Westchester County, New

Mary Reynolds Babcock, 1908–53, c. 1937

REYNOLDA HOUSE ARCHIVES
Ira L. Hill's Studio, New York City

York; or James Deering's Villa Vizcaya in Miami, perhaps—is no substitute for seeing the others. All are worth cherishing for what they tell of a past when some lived on a grand scale that has largely gone.

Reynolda is unique not only in its creation but also in its survival. The transformation from private estate to public institution began in the

1950s, and Reynolda's life as a museum is in some respects the most intriguing aspect of its history.

Reynolda is now both a home to a collection of American art and a house museum. Its walls are hung with noteworthy paintings and graphic art dating from the colonial period to the present, while the house retains the architectural features and most of the furniture with which the Reynolds family lived. There are also exhibitions of family memorabilia and cultural and educational events explicating the country-house era.

A shining star, the original Reynolda burned briefly. R. J. Reynolds's untimely death took Katharine Reynolds out of the large arena she might have enjoyed had her husband survived as one of the country's most important industrialists. Then her own death in 1924, just six years later, put an end to the founders' era.

Without its mistress, and with four children all under the age of eighteen, Reynolda drifted. In 1932 came the shocking death of the younger son, Zachary Smith Reynolds, four months before his twenty-first birthday. Whether he committed suicide, or the gun went off accidentally, or he was shot by his wife or his best friend has never been proven conclusively. The sensational coverage in the world's newspapers added an undercurrent of notoriety, and Reynolda remained in the shadows for several years, no longer the center of the family's life.

Reynolda awakened in 1935 when the elder daughter, Mary Reynolds Babcock, and her husband, Charles H. Babcock, bought it from the other heirs and refurbished it. They occupied Reynolda intermittently until 1948, when they moved there permanently.

In transmitting her love for Reynolda to her daughter, Katharine Reynolds ensured its survival for another generation. A question that preoccupied Mary and Charlie Babcock was how to preserve the house and its surrounding land beyond their lifetimes. The answer to this question arrived in stages. In the 1950s, thanks in part to their donation of 350 acres of Reynolda's land, Wake Forest College was able to relocate to Winston-Salem. The gardens were preserved by turning them over to the college in 1958. Reynolda Village was deeded to Wake Forest in 1965.

In 1964, the house began its transformation from private home to public institution under the guidance of Barbara Babcock Millhouse, Mary Babcock's daughter, whose dedication has played the major role in the evolution of Reynolda House into a museum of American art.

Through all their vicissitudes, this house and its landscape have retained a hold on Winston-Salem's imagination, first because R. J. Reynolds was the city's most successful citizen. The financial success of the R. J. Reynolds Tobacco Company brought prosperity matched by few other cities in the South. By the mid-1920s, his penchant for rewarding loyal employees and associates with company stock helped to create more than fifty millionaires in a city with a population of about sixty thousand.

Katharine Reynolds also was appreciated for her contributions to the city. She served a term as president of the YWCA, helped organize the Juvenile Relief Association, and founded the Junior League. She opened a progressive school on the grounds of Reynolda, and before the opening of R. J. Reynolds High School and Auditorium—to which she contributed both land and money—she arranged for local educational leaders (including herself) to tour cities in the Northeast to ensure that the school had the most up-to-date facilities.

Some of Reynolda's former acreage ultimately became one of Winston-Salem's finest residential neighborhoods, thereby influencing the course of the city's suburban development.

Reynolda's architect, Charles Barton Keen, and its landscape designer, Thomas Sears, went on to work extensively in the area. There are approximately twenty houses in Winston-Salem by Keen, who also designed R. J. Reynolds High School and Auditorium. Sears did much of the landscaping for these and other projects including one subdivision, becoming the city's favorite landscape designer.

Keen's influence spread beyond Winston-Salem to Greensboro and other North Carolina communities. Other designers adopted the formulas of Keen and Sears, and so the style in which they built has been even more widely reproduced.

While portions of Reynolda's story have been told, a full account has not been given. This book is a testament to the desire of Reynolda's board of directors for a more complete account and to the providence that allowed letters, bills, and other documents now part of Reynolda's archive to survive to reveal it.

Reynolda

A HISTORY OF
AN AMERICAN COUNTRY HOUSE

Chapter 1

BEFORE THE BEGINNING

On her tenth birthday, in November 1890, Katharine Smith received a gift of a gold bracelet from her forty-year-old second cousin, Richard Joshua Reynolds, who once jokingly promised to marry her someday. She spent the next twelve years growing up, while R. J. devoted himself to developing his business.

Their paths crossed again in a meaningful way in 1903. On March 12, eleven days after his seventy-eight-year-old mother died in bed at their home, R. J. wrote to Katharine, gently chiding her for not attending the funeral. After all, he reminded her, his mother was her paternal grandmother's sister and her great-aunt. "Your Winston relatives were disappointed in your not

stopping. . . . I hope you will arrange to come soon."

Less than a week later, R. J., now a bachelor of fifty-two, invited his niece Nannie Critz to accompany him to New York. Whether he suggested that Katharine join them or whether Nannie, her good friend, invited her is not known. But the trip gave R. J. an opportunity to observe Katharine as a young woman, and he must have liked what he saw, since an offer of a job as a secretary soon followed. She accepted and soon was one of three secretaries—the other two males—at his flourishing chewing-tobacco manufacturing company in Winston, North Carolina.

He had brought a whiff of excitement into her

life as a child. Now, R. J., whose reputed net worth of three million dollars made him one of the richest men in North Carolina, was making it possible for her to experience a wider world than that of her hometown of Mount Airy, North Carolina.

The relationship between the cousins blossomed, and on February 27, 1905, Katharine Smith and Richard Joshua Reynolds were married in an early-morning ceremony in her parents' parlor. The room was lavishly filled with roses, a gift from R. J. Immediately after the wedding, he whisked his bride away in a private railroad car bound for New York. The couple then embarked on a four-month European honeymoon.

Despite the difference in age, their union was a natural one. R. J. and Katharine's father, Zachary Taylor Smith, were good friends. Beyond family ties, R. J. and Katharine had geography and outlook in common. They grew up about forty miles apart, she in the North Carolina Piedmont, he in the hills of Virginia. Both were children of tobacco men in comfortable circumstances but not of great wealth, and both had been trained to find pleasure in a life of purpose. Both had a down-to-earth manner, a commanding presence, and a penchant for organizing enterprises and— it was said especially about Katharine—people.

There was no reason to imagine that they would build one of North Carolina's premier country estates, one that would endure as a legendary place of repose at the end of the twentieth century. But there was much in their personalities to indicate that any project they started would be carried out on a grand scale. Each welcomed challenges and had a progressive outlook. Most important, R. J.'s business success could provide the wherewithal to make an expensive undertaking like Reynolda possible.

He was descended from sturdy English stock. At his birth on July 28, 1850, R. J. was the second son of Hardin W. and Nancy Cox Reynolds. His parents went on to produce fourteen more children, eight of whom survived to adulthood. Growing up at Rock Spring Plantation in Patrick County, Virginia, he learned all aspects of the tobacco business. His father not only planted tobacco, but processed and sold it as well.

Hardin Reynolds operated a general store, lent out money at interest to his neighbors and friends, served as a commissioner for general elections and inspector of the county jail, and was the local postmaster. His taste for the finer things in life could be seen in his purchase of a rosewood piano for his wife and the books, pictures, and silverware that are still among the furnishings of his house. (The Reynolds homestead at Rock Spring is now a historic house museum, due mainly to the efforts of his granddaughter Nancy Reynolds.)

Hardin saw to it that his children got as much college education as they wished for, sending the girls to Salem Academy in Salem, North Carolina, and the boys to colleges in the area. R. J. was a student at Emory and Henry College in Virginia for two years, dropped out to work for a year, and later attended Bryant and Stratton Business College in Baltimore. When he joined his father in the tobacco business in 1873, he was following what in essence had been the family trade for at least three generations. He was well prepared for independent success when he turned over his share of his father's business to a younger brother and a cousin in 1874 and left to set up his own company in Winston. The attraction was Winston's new railroad. But the opportunity to be his own boss may have been equally appealing.

R. J. set up shop on a half-acre lot on Depot Street in a building measuring forty by sixty feet, which he purchased for $388.50. Hard work was his motto, and the rewards were financial success and the esteem of others. By the end of 1887, he had expanded his tobacco company several times over, acquired thirty-four tracts of land mainly in Winston, and become one of the city's solid citizens, his finger in many pies. As part of a syndicate, he bought and renovated the old Merchants Hotel and invested in a real-estate project at Mock's Mill in southeastern Virginia. He bought timberland and erected buildings in Winston,

which he rented out. He also involved himself in town affairs. The first time he ran for city commissioner, in 1879, he lost. Five years later, he was elected city commissioner and served as chairman of the sanitary and fire committees and supervisor of roads.

R. J.'s success permitted him to indulge in his favorite pastimes, one of which was the enjoyment of fine horses. He owned "the fleetest span of close matched mares in the south, if not the U.S.," according to one newspaper account. He also loved bird hunting. In 1887, he built himself a brick stable with seven stalls and space for feed and carriage storage. The stable was outfitted with a state-of-the-art water system that kept the water from freezing in winter. At a time when a good-sized house could cost under a thousand dollars, a local newspaper put the stable's cost at more than twenty-five hundred dollars, declaring it "no doubt the most complete stable building in the State."

R. J. was progressive in his political outlook. He signed a petition to tax property owners to pay for public schools, helped set up the Forsyth Five-Cent Savings Bank, and was well regarded by his employees, many of whom were blacks.

A fine figure of a man—he was over six feet tall—he had a host of friends in high and low places. He attended society balls and weddings but also sat in on poker marathons. Summing up the two sides of R. J., his brother Harbour described him in 1880 as "the biggest blood in Winston."

Katharine, born in 1880, would grow up to equal R. J. in initiative when she embarked on the planning of Reynolda. She was the eldest of seven children, and so came naturally by that tendency to organize others so often displayed by those who are first in the birth order. Her determination to excel was evident early. "She possesses a splendid intellect, does everything that she undertakes with credit to herself and a great satisfaction to her teachers," wrote her high-school principal in a letter of recommendation, in which he commended her as the best-prepared student ever to graduate from his school.

Though by no means as affluent as R. J. Reynolds, Zachary Smith was prosperous enough to provide his family a spacious house in the center of Mount Airy. A tobacco planter and owner of a tobacco auction warehouse, he also owned real estate and could afford a college education for his daughters.

When she took up R. J.'s offer of a job as one of his secretaries, Katharine had recently graduated from college and was living at home and earning a little pocket money by teaching china painting to ladies in town. Other girls destined for great marriages attended finishing school and learned flower arranging and French. Katharine matriculated at State Normal and Industrial College, a teachers' college for women in Greensboro, North Carolina (later the University of North Carolina at Greensboro), in preparation for teaching school and righting some of the wrongs of the world. A dynamic educational reformer named Charles D. McIver was president of the school, and he urged his students to "go forth into the State and endeavor to improve the condition of the people." Although she graduated from Sullins College in Bristol, Virginia, she spent her first three college years at McIver's school, then in the forefront of the movement for better education for women. No doubt, she would have graduated from that school if she had not contracted typhoid fever during an epidemic in her junior year. Though she recovered from the infection, the epidemic frightened her parents into transferring her to Sullins, where she could be near relatives living in Bristol.

Sometimes, those in her intimate circle found it hard to live up to Katharine's aspirations for them. Sixty years later, her roommate at State Normal, Emma Lewis Speight Morris, reminisced that Katharine had "a bit of a tendency to persuade people to do things for their own good." Katharine, who believed that sleeping with a pillow was unhealthy, would remove Emma's pillow whenever she saw it, until finally her roommate gave up using one.

Katharine once confided that she hoped to "go to Europe on my wedding trip . . . [and] bring home a wonderful work of art. . . . And then I shall buy a great estate . . . [and] have a thousand cattle on a hill . . . and flowers all around," as Morris recalled in an article in the college alumnae magazine. In 1905, not too many years after that girlish confidence, Katharine did go to Europe on her honeymoon. She brought home two artworks—portraits of herself and her husband which today hang in the reception hall at Reynolda House. A few years after the wedding, she was devoting her considerable energies toward creating the great estate complete with cattle and flowers.

HOME TO WINSTON

The magnificence they had seen in European cities must have seemed distant indeed when Katharine and R. J. Reynolds stepped from the train in downtown Winston in the summer of 1905, after their honeymoon. Farmers still brought the tobacco harvest to town in covered wagons. They camped out overnight near the tobacco sheds, cooking supper over open fires by the light of kerosene lanterns. Although it lacked the polish of a metropolis, Winston was a progressive Southern city. It led the world in the manufacture of chewing tobacco, also known as "flat plug," and produced smoking tobacco, too. Its 18,000 inhabitants in 1905 included 9,458 workers, more than 5,000 of whom worked in

the tobacco industry—many no doubt for R. J. Other industries—including textiles, brick and lumber processing, furniture making, and wagon making—also contributed to prosperity.

The city was small enough for a businessman to walk to work if he wanted to, perhaps stopping on the way to exchange the news of the day with acquaintances on street corners. Yet it was large enough to support thirty-one churches (eleven of them established by blacks), five public schools, a technical college for black students, two department stores with annual sales of almost three hundred thousand dollars each, a hotel, and an auditorium large enough to hold thirteen hundred people, according to a brochure published by the city's board of trade around 1905. The city also boasted excellent mail service, thanks to fourteen postal clerks, twelve city carriers, seven rural carriers, and six Railway Express clerks. There was a streetcar line with parks at its southern and northern termini, along with four railway lines offering eight daily arrivals and departures (some albeit strictly for freight). The Washington run took ten hours; the trip to New York required fifteen hours.

The Twin City Golf Club was at least eight years old in 1905, and its name was an indication of the ties between Winston and Salem. Although they would not be formally allied until 1913, already they were referred to as "the Twin City." Salem, founded in the eighteenth century by

Tobacco wagons in downtown Winston, c. 1905
REYNOLDA HOUSE ARCHIVES

Moravians who wanted to live according to their religious beliefs, was the sedate center of tradition. Winston, the booming new town born in 1851 as the seat of Forsyth County, was the engine whose economic might pulled both places toward development as a new type of Southern city based on industrial production rather than agriculture.

Katharine and R. J. settled down in R. J.'s spacious Queen Anne–style house at 666 West Fifth Street to enjoy life as one of Winston's first families. The large Victorian house with turrets and wraparound porch was less than a mile from his tobacco factory. Even though its plans had been supplied by a mail-order architect, a common practice in this period, it managed to be one of the most impressive houses in the nicest section of town—a neighborhood of substantial structures on tree-lined streets with broad front yards and backyard gardens.

Before his marriage, R. J. had shared the house with his mother, his younger brother Will, who worked at the tobacco plant, and Will's wife, Kate. Now, Will and Kate moved into a hotel, so the newly married couple had the house to themselves.

Construction of Queen Anne–style house at 666 West Fifth Street, c. 1893.
R. J. and Katharine Reynolds spent most of their married life here.

REYNOLDA HOUSE ARCHIVES

R. J. and Katharine Reynolds, her sister Maxie Dunn, unidentified woman,
and James Dunn on porch of Fifth Street house

REYNOLDA HOUSE ARCHIVES

While R. J. steered the company to new heights of prosperity, Katharine focused on bearing children, running her household efficiently, and participating in community organizations such as the YWCA. Besides the help of a cook, a laundress, a gardener, maids, nurses, and housemen, the family acquired a chauffeur when R. J. bought a Royal Tourist in 1907. Four children were born at regular intervals: Richard Joshua, Jr., in 1906, Mary in 1908, Nancy in 1910, and Zachary Smith in 1911.

Katharine smartened up R. J., taking charge of his wardrobe and insisting that he hire a valet. The man selected was John Carter, a black employee at the tobacco company who eventually became the major-domo at Reynolda House and stayed on the job until he died in the 1950s.

Parties at the house on Fifth Street were noted frequently in the local newspapers' society columns. There was, for example, the "colonial tea" Katharine gave in December 1906. Hostesses in full colonial garb—all of them members of the Daughters of the American Revolution—showed guests through a loan exhibit of "old colonial articles: old lace, silver, spreads, documents, old cut glass, firearms, etc." About a week later, the house was the setting for a "brilliant afternoon and evening." A band played behind the staircase in the hall, and guests circulated through various rooms that were decked out with elaborate floral

Major-domo John Carter (right) and his wife, Marjorie Carter, maid and later cook
REYNOLDA HOUSE ARCHIVES

arrangements, partaking of punch in the green-and-pink parlor, bonbons in cut-glass dishes in the dining room, and coffee and chocolate in the library.

Katharine Reynolds with Mary, Nancy, and Dick, c. 1911

R. J. Reynolds with Dick, Smith, and Mary, 1912

Katharine accompanied R. J. on business trips to New York, Philadelphia, and Baltimore, and the family traveled to the mountains of North Carolina to escape the steamy Winston summers, to Atlantic City (then a fashionable health resort), to the Florida coast, and to the Thousand Islands, on the border of the United States and Canada.

All of these activities were not enough to absorb her prodigious energies. Katharine also took an interest in the welfare of R. J.'s workers. Nannie M. Tilley, author of an encyclopedic history called *The R. J. Reynolds Tobacco Company*, has credited her with playing a role in the provision of drinking fountains, low-cost hot lunches, a nursery for the children of female workers, and housing for single white female workers.

What did R. J. think of his energetic young wife and her far-ranging interests? "I use [*sic*] to be happy, contented & much enjoyed being all alone at our house. . . . Now there is no pleasure in our beautiful house for me without you. I never dreamed such a change could be made in a short time," he wrote on August 18, 1909, to Katharine, who was summering in Roaring Gap, North Carolina. Two summers later, while she was pregnant with their fourth child, R. J. wrote to her at the Eseeola Inn in Linville, North Carolina, to remind her to "take the best care of yourself. My life would not be worth living without you." He sent her grapes and fresh vegetables while she was away from home. Once, after a visit from chocolate-bar manufacturer Milton S. Hershey of Pennsylvania, he sent a large quantity of Hershey's milk chocolate.

Katharine reciprocated his affection, as her anniversary letter to him in 1913 reveals. "Well, my sweetheart," she wrote from the Marlborough-Blenheim Hotel in Atlantic City, where she awaited him, "eight years ago, this morning we were starting out on life's journey together. . . . Today I'm far happier than I was even then; for at that time I feared it was too good to last. . . . Only one thing mars the day for me—your absence. . . . In these eight years, I believe, you, too, have been happier than you ever were before; and I trust I'll be able to make you happier in the next eight."

Chapter 2

ROMANCE OF THE LAND
1906-12

erhaps Katharine and R. J. developed an enthusiasm for rural living on the grand scale on their honeymoon in Europe, with its country "seats" with accessory villages belonging to the landed gentry. More likely, the ideas that went into the creation of Reynolda came out of the pages of American magazines. By 1906, when they made their first purchase of acreage, country estates for the affluent had become a national phenomenon, described in depth in publications subscribed to by Katharine: *Town & Country*, *Women's Home Companion*, and *Country Life in America*.

Reynolda's scale and features and the national panel of experts enlisted to bring it into being placed it on a different level from other farms in the North Carolina Piedmont.

R. J. knew at least one owner of a magnificent country place. He was James B. Duke, another tobacco tycoon. Duke headed the American Tobacco Company and between 1899 and 1911 owned a controlling interest in the R. J. Reynolds Tobacco Company. He resided in a luxurious Fifth Avenue mansion in New York and at Duke Farm in Somerville, New Jersey. The farm, which Duke began to develop in 1893, eventually encompassed twenty-two hundred acres. Its features included a half-mile racetrack for harness horses, a dairy herd of 250 registered Guernsey cows, and spectacular gardens filled with rare trees and flowers. Duke had lakes, bridges, and roads built on his land, and the landscaping firm that he employed—Buckenham & Miller of Somerville and New York—was the one Katharine and R. J. eventually called on to develop Reynolda's site plan and landscaping.

Then, too, there was Biltmore, George Vanderbilt's estate of 125,000 acres in Asheville, North Carolina, with its 255-room French "chateau" designed by Richard Morris Hunt, one of America's most distinguished architects. Biltmore, constructed between 1888 and 1895, dwarfed virtually every other country estate in the United States, and it served as a model for many of them. In August 1913, Katharine and R. J. attended a society horse show in Asheville with the Vanderbilts; that same year, she purchased landscaping plants from Biltmore. Katharine later entertained Vanderbilt's widow at Reynolda. She would also have known of Biltmore from articles, such as one in *House Beautiful* magazine in July 1903. The article, "A Millionaire's Village: An Ideal Village in the Hills of North Carolina, Designed As a Whole and Built to Order," glowingly described the village shops, dairy, school, and roads.

Katharine ultimately followed Vanderbilt's example in instituting model housing for her employees, as well as a noteworthy school and dairy. Like Vanderbilt and Duke, she developed a prize herd of cattle. Her wish to make Reynolda Farm a model of modern agricultural practices from which local farmers could learn was undoubtedly sincere. But she lived in an era when agriculture had become stylish among the rich. And Reynolda Farm was built in the image of other gentleman's farms around the country. Articles in *Country Life in America* regularly covered topics like the raising of prize cattle and poultry and the basics of greenhouse gardening. The magazine also reported on the efforts of estate owners in various parts of the country to elevate the local population. One article, for example, told of "a woman prominent in social circles in New York City [who] . . . made provision for courses of lectures on agricultural subjects like selection of better seeds and improved methods of farming."

Through advertisements in *Country Life in America* between April 1911 and April 1913—a critical period for the development of Reynolda—Katharine could have read about the "cream" of cream separators: "To the practical dairyman," the Vermont Farm Machine Company promised "profits. To the . . . 'home use' dairyman it means having the separator which is the *world's standard*." Poultry breeding stock, Guernsey and Jersey cows, landscape plants, and more were advertised regularly in the magazine.

R. J. supplied the funds, contributed his substantial expertise, and supervised the running of

Robert Holden (chauffeur), Katharine, son Dick, R. J., and nurse
on trip to Massachusetts in Royal Tourist (a right-wheel drive), 1907

the farm when Katharine was away or otherwise occupied. But it was she who managed the planning and building and who mainly communicated with the designers. Her name alone was on all of the deeds, and in recognition of her dominant role, the name of the property was legally changed in 1914 from Reynolds Farm, as it was first known, to the feminine Reynolda Farm. Altogether, she acquired twenty-two parcels of land totaling 1,067 acres. After 1906, when a 104.7-acre tract of farmland about two miles northwest of town was purchased, there was a break of three years before the next acquisition in 1909, of 336 acres in four separate parcels. By 1911, when numerous land-improvement and construction projects were under way, she owned about 660 acres. Later, she acquired about 400 acres for fields and orchards and 90 acres for polo fields and stables.

The deed books of Forsyth County reveal land costs of just under seventy-one thousand dollars. But some purchases were not valued or were valued at "one dollar and other considerations," so this figure is incomplete. Typically, parcels cost between fifty and a hundred dollars an acre. Some tracts were optioned by Katharine's brother-in-law James Dunn, a real-estate agent, possibly to keep the cost of the land down. The acreage included played-out farms, rugged hills, and woodland, some of it with beautiful views of the rural countryside. There also was plenty of pure drinking water—at least eighteen springs—an essential for a substantial agricultural community.

Katharine went about improving these assets with efficiency from her home on West Fifth Street, which she extensively remodeled in 1910, using the services of a Philadelphia-based decorating firm.

She visited Reynolda frequently, sometimes in the company of six lady friends. "We have a walking club now," Katharine wrote to a friend in June 1912. "We walk out to the end of my farm every morning and have an automobile to come out for us at ten o'clock. We wade in the branch, climb cherry trees, sit on the grass, play mumblepeg and have a good time in general." In summer, the family had large tents put up and comfortable furniture brought out and enjoyed hot meals prepared by its cook in an on-site outdoor kitchen.

THE FARM

The farm was central to the vision of Reynolda, and getting it in operating form was an early priority. Efforts at land clearing, road building, and soil improvement probably started as soon as each parcel was acquired. "Your farm looks fine covered with peas so high you could not see Dick if he was standing in your pea fields," R. J. wrote Katharine on September 16, 1910. "I

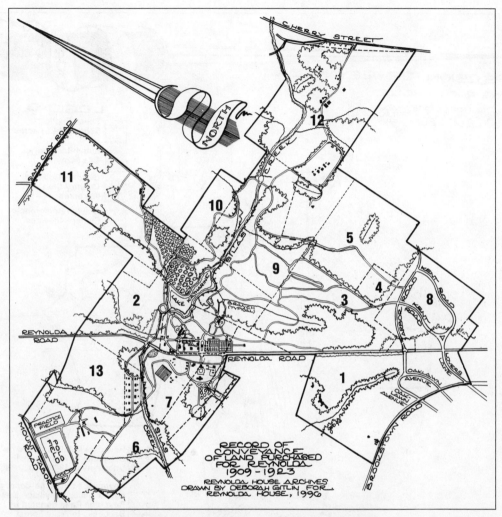

Record of Conveyance in order of date of purchase
(only property of ten acres or more listed)

1. Mary & O.B. Eaton, 104 acres, 1906
2. J.A. and H.A. Nading, 118 acres, 1909
3. Emory S. Gray, 79 + acres, 1909
4. Emory S. Gray, 10 acres, 1910
5. George D. Hodgin, 72 acres, 1909
6. Henry Reynolds heirs, 101 acres, 1909
7. Fannie J. Lee, (a widower of Harrisburg, Pa.)
   36 acres, 1909

8. W.H. Holleman heirs, 65 acres, 1909
9. M.H. & Grace Goins, 79 acres, 1910
10. H.W. Fries heirs, 24 acres, 1910
11. H.A. Nading, 95 acres, 1920
12. Ralph T. & Pearl Holbrook, 132 acres, 1920
13. J.K. Henning 87 acres, 1923

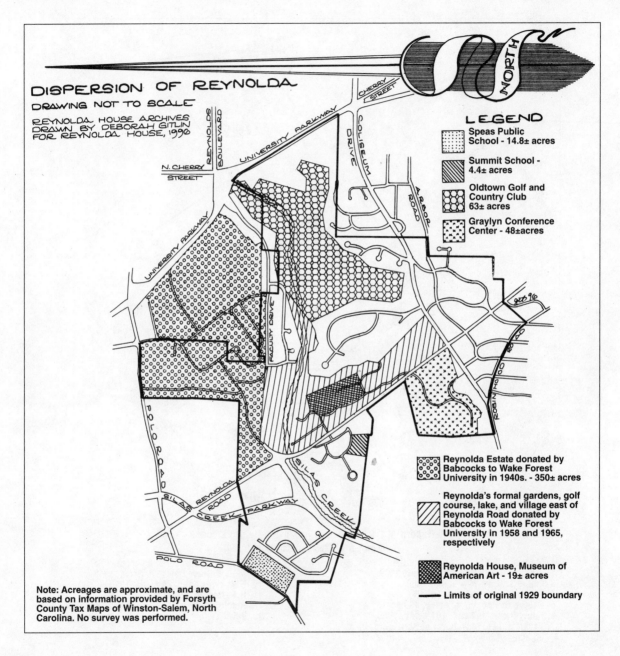

DISPERSION OF REYNOLDA

DRAWING NOT TO SCALE

REYNOLDA HOUSE ARCHIVES
DRAWN BY DEBORAH GITLIN
FOR REYNOLDA HOUSE, 1990

NORTH

LEGEND

Speas Public
School - 14.8± acres

Summit School -
4.4± acres

Oldtown Golf and
Country Club
63± acres

Graylyn Conference
Center - 48±acres

Reynolda Estate donated by
Babcocks to Wake Forest
University in 1940s. - 350± acres

Reynolda's formal gardens, golf
course, lake, and village east of
Reynolda Road donated by
Babcocks to Wake Forest
University in 1958 and 1965,
respectively

Reynolda House, Museum of
American Art - 19± acres

Limits of original 1929 boundary

Note: Acreages are approximate, and are
based on information provided by Forsyth
County Tax Maps of Winston-Salem, North
Carolina. No survey was performed.

am . . . having the well dug deeper at Hodgins place . . . [and] also having stable at Nading place moved to Hodgin farm. Bargained for teams to plow in your peas." In another letter the same month, he wrote to tell her that digging the Hodgin well deeper had not worked: "I am now looking for a well digger to sink a new well at the Hodgins farm. . . . Will start several hired teems [*sic*] to plowing in peas Monday. Could not get them earlier."

In 1910, in preparation for their projected golf course, they were also having land graded and improved and planting ryegrass. The farm already was supporting animals. "All of your horses mules cows & stock of every kind look well," R. J. wrote Katharine on September 22.

A farm manager named Fowler was hired for sixty-five dollars a month in the summer of 1911. On June 28, R. J. wrote from Fifth Street to tell Katharine, who was away in the mountains with the children, that the rock foundation for Lake Katharine's dam was in. He also indulged his love of teasing: "Tell Dick & Mary that their chickens crow so loud that I will have to eat them to keep from being disturbed early in the morning."

R. J. might joke about farm matters, but he was very well informed on their management and owned additional farms of his own. Katharine also

The governess Bum, Smith, unidentified women, and R. J. at Reynolda, c. 1914

REYNOLDA HOUSE ARCHIVES
Photographer unknown,
possibly Katharine Smith Reynolds

was knowledgeable about the technology of farming. Her interest was so great that she joined the North Carolina Conference for Social Service. That organization, founded by agricultural reformer Clarence Poe, worked to promote government policies and laws that would improve rural life in the state. Katharine served on the group's committees on improvement of country life and charities and benevolence.

In a letter indicative of their agricultural ambitions, R. J. wrote his wife on August 12, 1911, "I don't think Mr. Fowler has education enough for your farm & you should have a bigger man for the job than I think he will ever develop into. I have two educated farmers I am now investigating for the place." Eventually, she hired a graduate of the state agricultural college to manage the farm.

By 1912, the farm was in production. Katharine kept track of her experiment in

Unidentified woman, Nancy, Dick, Smith, R. J., and Mary camping
at Reynolda during construction of bungalow, c. 1915

REYNOLDA HOUSE ARCHIVES
Photographer unknown, possibly Katharine Smith Reynolds

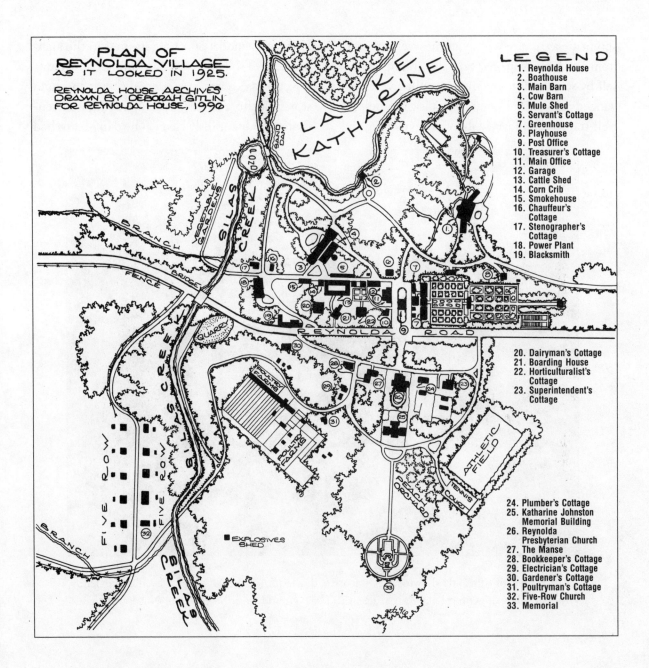

PLAN OF
REYNOLDA VILLAGE
AS IT LOOKED IN 1925.

REYNOLDA HOUSE ARCHIVES
DRAWN BY DEBORAH GITLIN
FOR REYNOLDA HOUSE, 1990

LAKE KATHARINE

LEGEND
1. Reynolda House
2. Boathouse
3. Main Barn
4. Cow Barn
5. Mule Shed
6. Servant's Cottage
7. Greenhouse
8. Playhouse
9. Post Office
10. Treasurer's Cottage
11. Main Office
12. Garage
13. Cattle Shed
14. Corn Crib
15. Smokehouse
16. Chauffeur's Cottage
17. Stenographer's Cottage
18. Power Plant
19. Blacksmith

20. Dairyman's Cottage
21. Boarding House
22. Horticulturalist's Cottage
23. Superintendent's Cottage

24. Plumber's Cottage
25. Katharine Johnston Memorial Building
26. Reynolda Presbyterian Church
27. The Manse
28. Bookkeeper's Cottage
29. Electrician's Cottage
30. Gardener's Cottage
31. Poultryman's Cottage
32. Five-Row Church
33. Memorial

SILAS CREEK
BRANCH
FENCE
BRIDGE
VEGETABLE GARDENS
QUARRY
REYNOLDA ROAD
FIVE ROW
FIVE ROW
SILAS CREEK
BRANCH
SILAS CREEK
POULTRY FARMS
EXPLOSIVES SHED
PEACH ORCHARD
ATHLETIC FIELD
TENNIS COURT

scientific agriculture by requiring weekly reports from her farm manager. She also informed herself by sending for government bulletins on advanced agricultural practices. With the help of well-trained employees, she was developing the farm into a model of progressiveness in the management of soil and crops and animal husbandry.

Reynolda's reinforced-concrete barns and grain storage facilities were fireproof, well lit, well ventilated, and spotlessly clean. The dairy barns had

Aerial view of Reynolda showing Reynolda Road, the formal gardens, and the village at left; the bungalow at center; Lake Katharine in the background; and the golf course at lower right

REYNOLDA HOUSE ARCHIVES
Aero Service of Philadelphia, c. 1927

Herd of Shropshire sheep grazing on golf course

REYNOLDA HOUSE ARCHIVES

Reynolda's Jersey herd

REYNOLDA HOUSE ARCHIVES

concrete floors, a state-of-the-art ventilation system, and individual drinking fountains for each cow. Milk and produce were stored in electric refrigerators, and the staff was expected to follow stringent safety rules—not doing so was grounds for dismissal—to keep the milk free of germs and untainted.

Public programs by the Forsyth County Extension Service on topics such as canning and cheesemaking were held at Reynolda's dairy. Katharine also sponsored "Corn Clubs," in which boys learned how to increase yields, and canning clubs for girls. These clubs, popular around the country, first appeared in the South around 1910 in South Carolina. Katharine wrote for information about them in 1912 and established them as part of the food-production efforts at her farm by 1917.

"The farm now has about 350 acres under cultivation," the *Twin City Sentinel* reported in July 1917. "The trucking interests are not small when one learns that there are [between] fifteen and twenty acres of beans, five acres in tomatoes, ten acres in sugar corn and several acres each in spinach, pumpkin and okra." The prospects looked bright: "Mrs. Reynolds declares that the future awaits the guinea raiser. They sell for a higher price than chickens and are strongly demanded by hotels and cafes of the north and east. . . . To raise guineas on a large scale would increase the fame of this section."

Dairy showing butter press in corner, bottling machine, churn, cream separator, and testing table

Foundation of dairy and retaining wall, built of rocks found on the property

Spillway dividing Lake Katharine and the concrete-bottomed pond

The Lake

One of Reynolda's most picturesque features was its sixteen-acre lake, created by damming Silas Creek and digging out a low-lying area, which was allowed to fill with water. The lake's depth was regulated by an arched spillway that emptied into a large, concrete-bottomed pond. A dam at one end of this concrete pond permitted the water level to be raised and lowered. The pond could be emptied to allow cleaning of the bottom and sides; one old-time resident recalled seeing men with brooms sweeping it out once a year when he was a boy.

The same fieldstones used in the foundation of the bungalow and various outbuildings were employed to face the poured-cement dam and the rustic stone bridge that passed over it. These stones, quite different from the angular fieldstones of New England, came from diabase rock that chipped off to create roughly rounded boulders. Using them made for a pleasing continuity in the landscape. The bridge, an excellent place for viewing the cascading waters of the spillway, became an entryway to the two-and-a-half-mile woodland road that circled the lake and wound through the woods and fields of Reynolda. On this picturesque thoroughfare, a rider or walker could make a circuit of a large portion of the property. In springtime when many thousands of daffodils were blooming, this dirt road was especially appealing.

The waters of Lake Katharine—which ultimately dried up as a result of the area's further development—were part of the life of Reynolda Village. Most seasons, there was fishing. In cold winters, there was ice skating. The concrete-bottomed pond below the spillway provided swimming facilities for people on the farm. Some former residents even recalled annual full-immersion baptism ceremonies there.

Boathouse on Lake Katharine, with roof of bungalow in background

Greenhouses, with Reynolda Presbyterian Church and manse in left background, c. 1919

REYNOLDA HOUSE ARCHIVES

THE FORMAL GARDENS

Horatio R. Buckenham and Louis Miller laid out the formal gardens in 1912 as part of Buckenham & Miller's general site plan for Reynolda. Katharine Reynolds later replaced this firm with Thomas Sears (1880-1965) of Philadelphia. Sears's first plans for Reynolda Gardens date from 1915. He created new architectural features and plantings, but the location, size, and contours of the formal gardens did not change from the Buckenham & Miller conception. The

association of Sears and Reynolda continued through the 1930s, when he revised the landscape for Mary Reynolds Babcock.

Why Katharine changed her landscaping firm intrigues those interested in American garden history, who have assumed that Sears was the brighter star. The name of Buckenham & Miller has faded from memory, while that of Sears has endured. But in 1912, Buckenham & Miller was considered the more distinguished firm. When the Children's Home of Winston hired Horatio R. Buckenham to survey and landscape its grounds in 1909, the September 21 issue of the *Winston-Salem Journal* referred to him as "the most noted landscape gardener in the world . . . [who] has made a fairyland of D. N. [*sic*] Duke's vast estate in New Jersey."

Between approximately 1905, when the firm was hired, and 1911, when it resigned from Duke's employ, Buckenham & Miller turned Duke's bland, flat farmland in Somerset County, New Jersey, into a wonderland of lakes, waterfalls, fountains, bridges, woodlands, and gardens. In addition to his work for Duke, Miller laid out other country estates, including one on the Gold Coast of Long Island for David Lamar, who was known as "the Wolf of Wall Street."

The employment of Sears may well have been suggested by Charles Barton Keen, whom Katharine hired at an unknown date, perhaps in 1911, to design Reynolda House and many of the other buildings. Keen had already collaborated with Sears on other country-house projects, and they were both located in Philadelphia.

Thomas Sears was one of the first college-trained landscape architects in the United States and a disciple of the new ideas about gardens that had flowed to these shores from Europe. He had impeccable credentials, having graduated from Harvard in 1903 and obtained a postgraduate degree in landscape architecture from Harvard's newly established Lawrence Scientific School in

1906. Even more important, he had worked for two years in the Boston office of Frederick Law Olmsted, Jr., and John Olmsted, the son and nephew of Frederick Law Olmsted, America's most eminent landscape designer.

A comparison of the surviving Sears planting plans with those that remain of Louis Miller's work shows that the Philadelphian followed Miller's ideas on the layout of the gardens but added his own special touches. Sears made changes in planting material and in the shape of some flower beds. For example, he substituted rectangular beds for Miller's rather tight-looking oval beds.

The formal gardens also were replete with architectural features designed by Sears, such as white-columned pergolas, brick steps and retaining walls, gravel walks, flagstone mowing paths, and water-lily pools, features that create interest any season of the year, in keeping with the best garden design of the period.

Reynolda's greenhouse complex, designed by Lord & Burnham, predated the arrival of Sears. The greenhouses were erected in the fall and winter of 1912–13. A domed building known as the Palm House occupied the center of the complex. Subsidiary structures included an orchid house, a vegetable house, a carnation house, a fern house, a rose house, and a unit referred to in plans as "general growing house #1."

The main door of the Palm House served as the chief public entrance to the four acres of formal gardens spread out beyond the greenhouses on a north-south axis. In the plans, the four acres were divided roughly in half between the Greenhouse Garden and the Nicer Vegetable and Flower Garden.

In the Greenhouse Garden, four symmetrical planting beds known as parterres were created by the construction of lengthwise and crosswise flagstone-edged grass lawns. Two of the parterres were devoted to roses; more than sixteen hundred rosebushes are believed to have been planted. The other two parterres were planted mainly with perennial flowers. Each had its own color theme. One contained blue and yellow flowers and the

The Palm House looking toward the formal gardens, c. 1919

other pink and white flowers. A grassy area was planted with weeping cherry trees. The central lawn that ran north-south through the Greenhouse Garden and terminated in a water-lily pool was planted with stately evergreen cryptomeria (Japanese cedar) trees.

Beyond the water-lily pool, wide, paved steps led up to a U-shaped structure consisting of three teahouses connected by pergolas. This architectural feature was itself the entrance to the Nicer Vegetable and Flower Garden, which was pleasingly planted with symmetrical beds of vegetables, flowers for cutting, grapevines, and fruit trees. At the end of the vegetable garden was a lawn planted with cedar trees and known as the Cedar Walk. This walk led to a log cabin that the boys used as a playhouse.

At one side of the Nicer Vegetable and Flower Garden, and overlooking it, was the girls' playhouse, a cottage consisting of a living room, bedroom, kitchenette, and bath, with ceilings about seven feet high. Designed by Keen to imitate an English thatched-roof cottage, the playhouse bears a marked similarity to another cottage of his done

Water-lily pool framed by teahouses and pergolas, c. 1919

33

Main axis of vegetable garden looking
toward greenhouses, with power-plant
smokestack in background, c. 1919

referred to the "Italian Garden," while others
spoke of the "English Garden."

The journalists may have been confused, but
the garden planners were not. American country-house builders and their landscape architects
wanted to create formal Italian (or European)
gardens and naturalistic English vistas on the same
property. In doing so, they formulated a new syn-
thesis that was not necessarily historically accurate but that offered the best of two garden worlds.
European formal gardens were based on ideas of
symmetry begun in the Renaissance and perfected
in the eighteenth century. The English idea—developed at country houses in the seventeenth and

for an estate in Cedarhurst, New York. Although
about the same size as a real bungalow of the early
twentieth century, the playhouse appears minia-
ture in comparison to Reynolda House nearby.
The Lilliputian impression is emphasized indoors
by kitchen counters that come up to an adult's
hips and a bathtub only four feet long. It was just
right for preteen girls. Supervised by one of their
teachers, the Reynolds girls and their cousins and
girlfriends frequently spent the night here.

The symmetrical arrangement of Reynolda's
formal gardens was reminiscent of gardens in eighteenth-century Italy and France. Indeed, some
published accounts of Katharine's garden parties

The girls' playhouse, with roof
designed to look like thatch, c. 1919

Cryptomeria allée looking toward the Palm House, 1919

35

Formal gardens showing main pergola, c. 1919

eighteenth centuries—was to create a natural-looking paradise in which landscape features, rather than formal flower beds, were emphasized.

Like other gardens at early-twentieth-century American estates, Reynolda's gardens had their exotic elements, including Oriental touches in the cryptomeria trees and weeping cherries and the Japanese-inspired teahouses built of cypress wood.

Reynolda's gardens were located to the west of the house, well beyond the view of its main public rooms. When trees were in full leaf, the gardens could only be glimpsed from rooms on the western side of the house. At most country estates, formal gardens could be seen from the main rooms, so this choice at first seems a puzzle. One reason it was done this way, as suggested years later by Nancy Reynolds, was that her mother wanted to share the gardens with the community while still maintaining some privacy for herself. She certainly did share them. In 1917, ten thousand people came to see the gardens, according to an account in a local newspaper.

The garden site was excellent in relation to the greenhouse complex. From the Palm House, the sunken Greenhouse Garden (several steps down) spread out in a magnificent show. The vantage point of the Palm House also showed off to best advantage the ornamental pool and the teahouses and pergolas which marked the termination point of the first garden.

In Katharine's time, when many gardeners were available to do the constant maintenance required to keep the lawns and the many beds in perfect order, the display from the Palm House must have been breathtaking.

THE VILLAGE

The entrance to Reynolda Village was marked by a massive stone water trough off a main north-south thoroughfare in Winston-Salem now known as Reynolda Road but then referred to as Bethania Road or Yadkinville Road.

Katharine Reynolds paid to have concrete laid for the mile-and-a-half portion of road near

View from village entrance across Reynolda Road to water trough, post office,
and greenhouse at right and treasurer's house at left, c. 1912

Reynolda. The section was said by the *Twin City Sentinel* in 1917 to be the first concrete road in the state.

With the exception of Reynolda Presbyterian Church and its immediate grounds, which Katharine deeded to the congregation in 1915 after paying for the church's design and construction, she owned all the land in view on both sides of the road. Designed by Keen, the church had half-timbered gables and stained-glass windows by D'Ascenzo Studios, a Philadelphia firm that later made windows for the Cathedral of St. John the Divine in New York. The church was placed on the western side of the road, along with a manse and six substantial cottages for supervisory employees.

The main part of the village was located on the eastern side of the road. There were two focal points in this section: the greenhouse complex and the group of gleaming white stables, dairy barns, and silos set on a hill overlooking the village. Other buildings included a power plant, a schoolhouse, workshops, garages, employees' houses, a post office, the superintendent's office, servants' quarters, and a blacksmith shop with a forge.

Virtually all of the buildings, including the church and cottages across the road, were white

Looking north on Reynolda Road, c. 1919

Post office at village entrance, with greenhouses on right

Presbyterian Church, with manse at right, c. 1919

REYNOLDA HOUSE ARCHIVES

Outdoor auditorium behind church during
wedding of R. J.'s niece Senah Critz and Charles A. Kent, 1918

REYNOLDA HOUSE ARCHIVES

Dairy barns, stables, and silos set on a hill overlooking the village

REYNOLDA HOUSE ARCHIVES

with green roofs, in common with the main house. Many shared other features with Reynolda House, such as Tuscan-inspired white stucco columns and low-ridged roofs from which chimneys of native rounded stones rose. The same stones were used for foundations and low walls. Indeed, even Five Row, the small, separate hamlet of whitewashed wood-frame houses for black families, located about a half-mile from the main village complex, fit into the overall pattern of white buildings in a green landscape.

The Reynolda Village buildings look traditional today but were no doubt thought of as modern when constructed. Their simple roofs and columns, their lack of fussy ornament, and their white walls and green roofs gave them an appearance quite different from the irregular, picturesque forms preferred by the previous generation. The buildings also were equipped with the latest technology. The estate had its own coal-powered power plant, water system, steam heating system, telephone lines, and sewage and sanitation systems. The pipes and wiring ran underground in tunnels of concrete and terra cotta that connected many of the buildings of the estate. These subterranean hallways, lit by electric lights, were large enough for a grown person to walk through.

Power plant

REYNOLDA HOUSE ARCHIVES
Copy print from a photo owned by Al Drage

Blacksmith shop, with
dairy, silos, and cow barns
in background, c. 1919

REYNOLDA HOUSE ARCHIVES
Copy print from a photo owned by Al Drage

REYNOLDA AS A COMMUNITY

More than a hundred workers were required to build Reynolda, Katharine Reynolds told a newspaper interviewer in 1917. Approximately the same number of employees worked on the estate after it was completed—tending its crops, dairy, farm animals, greenhouses, and gardens and keeping the house in a state of perfection.

While some employees undoubtedly came from town and the surrounding farms (including some of the domestics, for there were no servants' quarters at Reynolda House), many lived on the property. The estate's superintendent, treasurer, stenographer, horticulturist, gardener, dairyman, poultryman, electrician, plumber, bookkeeper, and chauffeur all had houses or cottages which they and their families occupied in Reynolda Village. There was also a building, known as the Servants' Quarters, where domestic workers at the bungalow could rest, shower, change clothes, or spend the night if they had to.

The *Twin City Sentinel* reported on July 7, 1917, "Reynolda [Village] is a happy community. It is formed of about twenty resident families, each allotted a garden plot for their own personal use with the privilege of cultivating as they will."

Garden plots were only one advantage of life in Reynolda Village. Residents were free to enjoy most of the facilities of the estate, including the golf course (rarely used by the family) and the tennis courts. They could also swim in the concrete-lined pond adjoining the lake and boat, fish, and ice-skate on the lake itself. Most of them attended Reynolda Presbyterian Church. Some hired the wives of the farmworkers living at Five Row to do part-time cleaning and laundering.

J. Alfred Drage, Reynolda's horticulturist, in canoe on Lake Katharine

REYNOLDA HOUSE ARCHIVES
Copy print from a photo owned by Al Drage

Contractors and construction crew on lake porch of bungalow, c. 1916

They could even peruse the latest magazines and farm journals, which were available in a reading room in the superintendent's office.

Keen designed or supervised the design of the cottages and equipped them with all the modern conveniences. "The cottages are attractive in design, and also attractively decorated inside and out," the *Sentinel* continued. "Each family may secure milk from the dairy and vegetables from the farm at wholesale cost."

In return for a beautiful, comfortable, and free place to live, workers were expected to keep the premises neat. Katharine Reynolds made frequent inspection trips of the grounds, usually on her horse, Kentucky Belle, and exacted small fines if she found things out of order. "Fifty cents if she found anything in the window [like] maybe a dishcloth or anything that shouldn't be in a window when she's driving around showing off things," recalled Lucy Hadley, one of the teachers who lived on the property.

Families such as the Robert Gibsons enjoyed the easy, informal style of life and the attractive environment. Gibson and his wife and daughter

Nadeina Gibson, daughter of electrician Robert Gibson, on tricycle at cottage of superintendent Clint Wharton

REYNOLDA HOUSE ARCHIVES
Photograph by Thomas Sears

Cottage of electrician Robert Gibson, later the plumber's cottage

REYNOLDA HOUSE ARCHIVES
Photograph by Thomas Sears

were one of the first families to move into the new cottages at Reynolda. They arrived either in 1914 or 1915, when Gibson was hired to install and maintain many of the electrical and telephone systems. Mrs. Gibson took odd jobs around Reynolda, helping with the switchboard at the main house, providing lunch for the dairymen, and lodging visiting workmen such as the Otis Elevator inspector. The Gibsons' daughter, Nadeina, enjoyed tea parties with Nancy Reynolds; on rainy days, the two girls played dress-up in Reynolda's attic. Years later, Nadeina Gibson Buchanan recalled with pleasure the beautiful clothing that Katharine passed along to Nadeina's mother.

The little settlement known as Five Row was home to many of Reynolda's black farmworkers. Five Row encompassed ten houses and a building that served jointly as a church and school, according to a plan of the estate made in 1925.

"When we moved there, there were five houses [in a row], and that is how come we called it Five Row," said Flora Pledger, who was living there with her husband, a farmworker, by 1917. If there was a reason for the name other than the one Flora suggested, it has been lost. There is no

Flora Pledger and Lilly Hamlin, Five Row residents

known written record of the early days of Five Row, and except for the building housing the church and school, which was moved to another site, the community was torn down to make way for Silas Creek Parkway in the early 1950s.

The first people to settle at Five Row, according to community recollection, were Will Ward and his wife, Betty. Ward worked at land clearing and ditch draining. Before moving to Five Row in 1914, he made the trip by foot from his home in Bethania, several miles away. But even before the Wards came, three boardinghouses served as temporary housing for male workers engaged in clearing the land. From such beginnings, Five Row developed into a full-fledged community by the time Reynolda was completed in 1917.

The houses to which the farmworkers were assigned faced one another across a tree-shaded lane. The simple white-painted frame structures each had a front and rear porch. Like other residents living away from the village center, Five Row residents had neither running water nor electricity. But the solidly constructed four- and five-room houses were considered a good place to live. During Katharine's lifetime, tenants paid no rent. Later, a nominal sum from $.50 to $1.50 a week was collected.

Religion was central to the lives of many Five Row residents, who organized the Reynolda Missionary Society and the Reynolda Prayer Band as religious, charitable, and social outlets. Sunday services were held in the combination schoolhouse and church. Weekdays, the same building offered classroom instruction through the seventh grade.

Most of the blacks at Five Row came from rural areas. At Reynolda, they did the kind of work they had known all their lives. The men mowed fields, hauled coal, did roadwork, cleaned drains, or trimmed trees. The women who worked (a number stayed home to care for their children) were laundresses, cooks, or housemaids.

There were many opportunities for part-time work. Teenage boys were hired to sweep roads with push brooms, mow, pull crab grass, sell Reynolda's surplus vegetables at a stand in the city market, and deliver milk from the dairy to various customers. An enterprising youngster such as Harvey Miller, who grew up at Five Row and eventually became Mary Reynolds Babcock's butler, could find quite a variety of part-time jobs. As a boy, Harvey baby-sat and washed windows for Robert Conrad, the head gardener. He worked at the garage, where the black chauffeur, George Wharton, "would pay me himself to wash the cars." He sold Reynolda's salad dressing from door to door, helped with haying in late summer and early fall, and did odd jobs for Reynolda's cook. She "would always give me something . . . to-mato pudding or a lamb sandwich . . . ," he re-

Thomas Warren in front of Five Row schoolhouse

small prizes such as ribbons for the prettiest garden. Those who wanted them could obtain seeds or plants from the Reynolda greenhouses. Many residents kept vegetable gardens, where they grew their own food. Harvey Miller's family and the Pledgers cooperated on a big vegetable garden; each spring, Miller's father brought a Reynolda team to plow the joint garden. Some people kept hens for eggs and raised chickens, and a few even had a dairy cow. They also could buy produce and a piglet from Reynolda at low cost. As a boy, Harvey Miller was given a calf from the Reynolda herd to raise for himself. "Maybe it wasn't as trimmed as she [Katharine] liked or had a bad knee or something, or maybe it was a little large, but I thought it was a beautiful calf," he recalled.

"THE HOME PLACE"

In her will, Katharine Reynolds referred to Reynolda House and the 136 acres surrounding it as "the home place." To her, and no doubt to most other people, this homeplace was the centerpiece of Reynolda Estate.

A road up the hill from Reynolda Village led to the house, but visitors were more likely to make use of the separate entrance about half a mile closer to town. They drove through imposing iron gates set into massive stone pillars and made their way down a long macadam drive skirting the golf

membered. "Everything that come from the bungalow was wonderful."

Objectively, black workers at Reynolda in the early years did at least as well there as in the jobs they would have been able to get as unskilled factory workers. They earned almost as much as tobacco workers and received free housing and benefits such as access to free or low-cost food and a pleasant rural environment.

Katharine Reynolds, who rode over to Five Row on Kentucky Belle two or three times a week, encouraged residents to grow flowers by giving

course and winding gently through a thick grove of trees. A right turn took them into the forecourt of the house, while the road continued down the hill past the gardens and into the village.

The grounds surrounding the house offered a variety of outlooks and moods. A porte-cochere over the main entrance on the south side of the house was festooned in summer with Silver Moon climbing roses. The view from the porte-cochere was toward the golf links, whose eighth tee was marked by a native persimmon tree that still stands in its original location.

On the north side of the house, wisteria vines were trained on the Tuscan columns of the semicircular lake porch. Just below the porch, and echoing its graceful, rounded edge, were wide steps leading to electrically lighted paths down to the tennis courts and an ever-flowing natural swimming pool filled from an artesian well. Climbing red roses were planted on the wire fence surrounding the tennis courts, which were overlooked by a rustic pavilion. A stream ran alongside the swimming pool, and an arched stone bridge over it led to the lake road. Also on the north, and visible from inside the house through a large plate-glass window in R. J.'s study, was a small, circular garden with a round pool and a fountain. Rhododendrons and azaleas were planted here, as well as ferns and Madonna lilies.

Stone pillars marking the south entrance to Reynolda

Lake porch, with wisteria vines
trained along trellis
REYNOLDA HOUSE ARCHIVES
Photograph by Thomas Sears

Porte-cochere festooned with
climbing roses, with open-air
sleeping porch above
REYNOLDA HOUSE ARCHIVES

49

Vista toward Lake Katharine from bungalow

REYNOLDA HOUSE ARCHIVES
Photograph by Thomas Sears

Outdoor swimming pool, with
Lake Katharine in background

REYNOLDA HOUSE ARCHIVES

Terrace garden planted with rhododendrons and azaleas, north side of east wing

A Vision In White

From the house on the knoll above the lake, the village, its barns and house rooftops, and meadows could be seen in the distance. In any direction, it was a vision of peace and plenty.

Now that most of the land is used for other purposes, the house has come to dominate Reynolda's history. But it was the whole estate, rather than one of its parts, that was Katharine's great achievement.

The harmony and coherence of the entirety were emphasized by the use of white stucco or wood and green roofs. The whiteness contributed to the feeling that Reynolda was a place apart.

Perhaps the most famous American "village" of white buildings was the one created for the 1893 World's Columbian Exposition in Chicago. With its giant orders executed in plaster, the exposition, known as "the White City," fascinated those who visited it. As one commissioner said in awe, "Oh gentlemen, it is a dream." This dream continued to exert its influence even after the turn of the century, whenever the American imagination turned toward utopian development. Whether "the White City" of 1893 resonated in the mind of either Charles Barton Keen or Katharine Reynolds can only be conjectured, but they would have been quite familiar with it.

Chapter 3

REYNOLDA HOUSE TAKES SHAPE

1912-17

K atharine and R. J. Reynolds referred to their new house as "the bungalow," even though the richly appointed interiors, sixty-four rooms, and additional service areas were well beyond the modesty of a bungalow, as the term is typically understood.

The plan of Reynolda House encompassed a four-story main section and two wings, each attached to the main block at a twenty-degree angle. The real height of the house could be seen at its rear and sides. But in its long, low roofline and recessed porches, the central block of Reynolda House gave the impression of being an extra-large bungalow from the front.

Katharine and R. J.'s preference for the word

bungalow demonstrated their unpretentiousness, their desire for an informal home, and their familiarity with the ideals of the American Arts and Crafts Movement, whose leaders glorified the bungalow as the proper kind of house in which to bring up healthy and robust children.

Because of its size and its Colonial Revival details, Reynolda House cannot be considered an orthodox example of the Arts and Crafts style. But the architect, Charles Barton Keen (1868–1931), was quite familiar with the design doctrines of the Arts and Crafts Movement. During his early career, Keen had taken night courses in drawing at the Pennsylvania Museum and School of Industrial Art, a stronghold of Arts and Crafts

Charles Barton Keen (1868–1931),
architect of Reynolda

thinking founded in the 1870s in emulation of the Kensington Museum and School in London, also a center for the Arts and Crafts philosophy.

As one of a group of Philadelphia architects with national reputations who specialized in country estates, Keen designed houses that were commodious, comfortable, and even luxurious without being overly pretentious. He had studied architecture at the University of Pennsylvania, graduating in 1889 with a command of historical architectural styles. Then he spent three years as a draftsman in the offices of two influential Philadelphia architects, after which he enjoyed the benefits of a grand tour through the capitals of Europe and the Orient.

The young architect's career certainly wasn't hurt by the associations he made. He worked first as a draftsman for Theophilus P. Chandler (1845–1928), the first dean of Penn's architecture school, and later for Frank Miles Day (1861–1918), one of the founders of *House and Garden* magazine. Keen's drawings were regularly exhibited at annual shows of the influential T-Square Club of Philadelphia. And when Day, Wilson Eyre, Jr., and Herbert C. Wise started *House and Garden* in 1901, they published Keen's design of Stratford Lodge, a country house in Bryn Mawr, Pennsylvania, in the first issue.

By the time Katharine Reynolds engaged him in 1911 or 1912, the architect had achieved national recognition. He had built numerous country estates and farms in America's affluent suburbs. His most famous project, a country house at Saratoga Springs, New York, for the actor Chauncey Olcott, had been widely featured in national magazines devoted to home decoration. Several of his houses were illustrated in *The Country House* by Charles Edward Hooper, a 1909 book that is in the Reynolda House library and almost certainly belonged to Katharine Reynolds.

There is no record of how Keen and Katharine

Deck running along crest of roof to lower height of bungalow

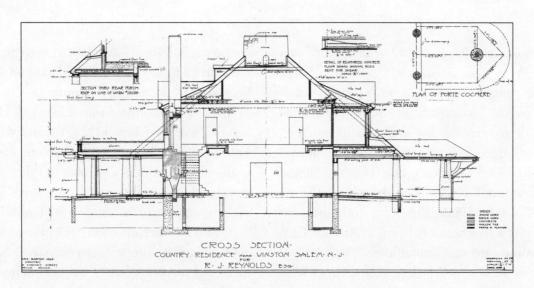

Cross section of house from architectural plans

Plan by Charles Barton Keen

The bungalow, c. 1917

Reynolds met, but it might have happened in a variety of ways. Architects and country-house clients usually found one another through social and business connections, and the Reynoldses had friends and business ties in Philadelphia. R. J.'s advertising agency (the N. W. Ayer Company) and Katharine's decorating firm (Hunt, Wilkinson & Company) were both in the city. Katharine and R. J. visited Philadelphia frequently and spent weeks at a time at luxury hotels in Atlantic City, a favorite watering spot of affluent Philadelphians who might have put the lively couple from Winston in touch with the sociable and charming architect. Keen designed a new house in Winston for Robert E. Lasater in 1912; Lasater, a vice presi-

dent at the R. J. Reynolds Tobacco Company who was married to R. J.'s niece, could have provided Keen an introduction to Katharine.

The design and construction of Reynolda House occupied five years, from 1912 to the end of 1917. This was unusually long, since the house was not nearly as elaborate as a number of others built more quickly around the same time. World War I was responsible for some delays. The United States did not formally enter the war until 1917, but the conflict disrupted American trade before then, and surviving letters mention difficulties in obtaining materials and finding qualified workers because of the war. Of course, Keen also was designing other buildings on the estate, and

Katharine frequently was preoccupied by other aspects of the project and by R. J.'s illness beginning in the summer of 1917.

Since client and architect were geographically separated in an era before the telephone was the standard means of communication, they kept in touch by letter. Unfortunately, the correspondence between them for important years such as 1914 and 1915 has not survived. The letters that do exist reveal a cordial working relationship despite Katharine's occasional impatience when plans were delayed. "I had counted on you, Mr. Keene [sic] making the plans for stables, dairy, garage, etc . . . and these are what we are needing so much at present," Katharine wrote on July 5, 1912. She wrote to a friend on July 26 that it "seems almost impossible for Mr. Keene to complete our plans."

Keen acted as general contractor, while a succession of on-site superintendents saw to day-to-day operations. Katharine Reynolds was, however, involved in every decision. She set up a home office at Fifth Street and employed a secretary, who came in to take dictation, type letters, and file.

In the early phases of planning, Katharine and Keen wrote back and forth on issues such as where to locate the trunk room and how large to make the coalbin. She appears to have taken few, if any, of Keen's recommendations on faith. She

vetoed the size of the horse stalls he proposed in favor of smaller stalls and even insisted that a barn weather vane be changed to more accurately represent a Jersey cow.

What Style Is The House?

The design of Reynolda House was far from a direct copy of any style that preceded it. The building's low roofline, its thick, tapered columns, and the foundation of rough, rounded fieldstones called to mind some large barns erected in the Pennsylvania countryside by German immigrants beginning in the eighteenth century. The way in which the structure was tied to its landscape bespoke the influence of reform-minded English architects such as Richard Norman Shaw (1831–1912) and C. F. A. Voysey (1857–1941). The distinctive angled wings had a precedent in the whimsically termed butterfly manor houses that enjoyed a brief vogue in Edwardian England.

Although Reynolda House included English and American vernacular features that conveyed a feeling of tradition, it was a house of its time, neither breaking new ground as later modernist houses would do nor duplicating a specific design of the past. Well-trained architects like Keen knew how to combine eclectic elements without allowing their design to go out of control. The combinations such architects devised would never have occurred historically, but they conveyed a pleasing sense of tradition and dignity. Their further goal was to satisfy their clients' demand for fine construction and craftsmanship and for modern improvements such as electricity, tiled bathrooms, and central vacuum-cleaning systems. Reynolda, like a number of country houses of its era, was built of reinforced concrete and hollow tiles, which made it fireproof and virtually indestructible.

FROM PLAN TO REALITY

Reynolda House went through at least one major change of design. A plan dated July 15, 1912, shows a house with a main block and a single short wing. A revised plan of September 25, 1912, presents the house close to the way it was actually built, with its two angled wings.

The plans in Reynolda's archive tell the story of the house's construction timetable. Structural diagrams mainly date from 1912 and 1913. The superstructure went up in this period. Room plans date from 1914 and 1915, when the interior took shape. There are many diagrams of interior details such as bookcases, ceiling grills, and refrigerator doors from 1916 and 1917, when interior finishing was the focus of the work.

The heart of the house was (and is) its thirty-eight-by-forty-seven-foot reception hall. A true

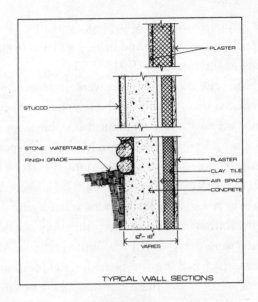

Bungalow wall section of
reinforced concrete and hollow tile
Drawn for Reynolda House by Edwin Bouldin

"living hall," this room was not only the largest and most impressive in the house but also the main gathering place for family and guests and a space through which everyone had to pass. The reception hall was also the musical center of the house, since the Aeolian pipe organ was heard to best advantage here.

Living halls, which derive in part from Elizabethan manor houses, made their first appearance in American homes in the second half of the nineteenth century. One of the first living halls was in a house designed by H. H. Richardson,

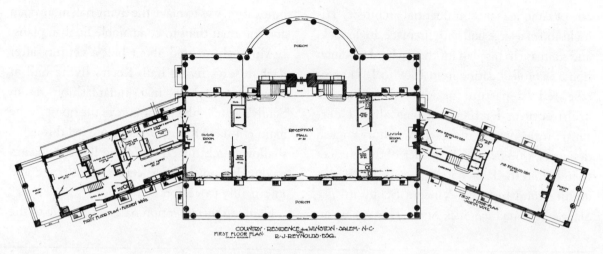

First-floor plans, 1919

REYNOLDA HOUSE ARCHIVES
Traced from Charles Barton Keen's drawings by J. E. Ellerbe

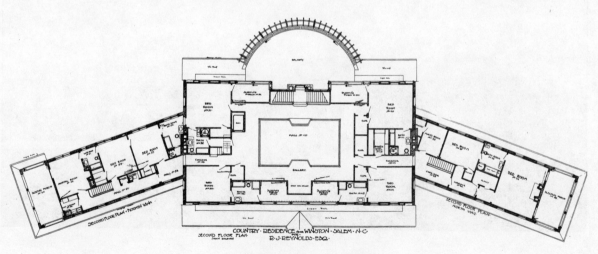

Second-floor plans, 1919

REYNOLDA HOUSE ARCHIVES
Traced from Charles Barton Keen's drawings by J. E. Ellerbe

one of America's most influential architects. His inclusion of a large hall with fireplace, inglenook, and staircase in his plan for the Richard Codman house (a project dating from 1869 to 1871) represented a departure for American domestic architecture. Richardson was almost certainly influenced by nineteenth-century English designers, who reworked the idea of the Elizabethan hall in the late 1850s and early 1860s, says architectural historian Vincent Scully in *The Shingle Style and the Stick Style*. The American innovation was to make the living hall more open and informal than in comparable English plans.

Although created about half a century after Richardson's living hall, Keen's living hall at Reynolda functioned in a similar fashion—as, in Scully's words, "the living core of the house." The main entrance to Reynolda House led through a shallow porch directly into the living hall, immediately conveying a feeling of welcome and informality to visitors.

Flanking the reception hall and leading to the

Bungalow under construction, c. 1915–16

Reception hall, c. 1918

REYNOLDA HOUSE ARCHIVES

Sun porch running
along the front facade

REYNOLDA HOUSE ARCHIVES

west wing was a formal dining room. Beyond the dining room were a serving pantry, a walk-in vault for silver storage, and a family kitchen used by Katharine Reynolds and her daughters and their friends to make fudge and prepare snacks. This wing also included rooms used by the staff, the children, and their caretakers during the day.

To the east of the reception hall was a living room, which in turn led to the east wing, in which were situated individual dens for Katharine and R. J.

Opposite the long front entrance porch, a large, semicircular rear porch with a tile floor overlooked Lake Katharine. Canvas panels at the edge of the lake porch could be lowered against wet or cold weather to turn the space into an outdoor living room. A fireplace further extended the utility of this area.

The second floor, devoted to spacious bedrooms and baths and plenty of closets, included a "hospital room," where individuals in a contagious state could be isolated to protect the welfare of

Living room, with door to Katharine's den to left of fireplace, c. 1918

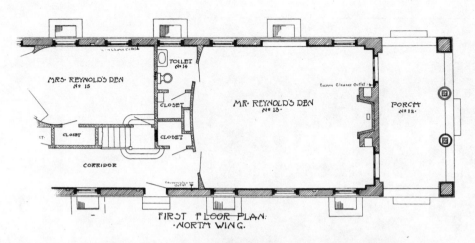

Plan of Katharine's and R. J.'s dens in east wing, 1919.
Although the plan shows a door from the stair landing, it was never built.

REYNOLDA HOUSE ARCHIVES
Traced from Charles Barton Keen's drawings by J. E. Ellerbe

Katharine's den, c. 1918
A partition was built dividing this room
in the 1936 renovation.

REYNOLDA HOUSE ARCHIVES

Semi-circular lake porch, c. 1918
REYNOLDA HOUSE ARCHIVES

others. Fresh air was considered an essential element in preserving health, and off each bedroom was a sleeping porch furnished with beds. There was also an unusual second-floor terrace with a tile floor. This outdoor space was actually the roof of the first-floor lake porch. In the interest of safety, a parapet at waist height surrounded the space. A festive touch was provided by the planters that lined the parapet.

It took quite a bit of utility space to run a complex house like Reynolda, and the attic and basement were given over to the task. Besides its role as a storage area, the attic accommodated a portion of the working parts of the organ, whose pipes rose behind a tapestry from the second floor. In the basement were the main kitchen, with its mammoth coal and gas stoves, as well as service areas and space for the house's mechanical systems. In the kitchen area were a serving room, a storeroom, a maids' dining room with a porch, and men's and women's toilets. Near the back door were a package receiving room, a full bathroom, the elevator and its machinery, and a toolroom that led into an area containing an early type of air cooler. The basement also included spaces for the boiler, the hot-water storage tank, and the coalbin.

The final plans show that Reynolda House was equipped with two kitchens and a pantry, three dumbwaiters, an elevator, fourteen bathrooms, a telephone in every room, electric lighting (including closet lights that went on whenever the closet door was opened), and the pipe organ, among many other details indicating the modernity of the house and the superiority of its workmanship.

After the house was completed, Keen put its cost at two hundred thousand dollars, an exceedingly rough figure since it did not include the cost and installation of utilities, the elevator, the dumbwaiters, and the kitchen stove and other major appliances. Neither did it include the cost of furnishings or land. Today, of course, the house would cost millions of dollars to build.

Originally, the budget was less than half of the two hundred thousand dollars. Seeking bids from contractors, Keen advertised the house in the July 3, 1912, edition of the *Philadelphia Real Estate Record and Builder's Guide* as a seventy-five-thousand-dollar structure of two and a half stories with a tile roof, electric lighting, and central heating.

Katharine may not have intended for her house to cost quite so much as it did. The normally generous owner of Reynolda refused a relative's request for a loan in 1918 with the comment that she regretted "exceedingly that I am not in a position to accommodate you. . . . My expenses [on Reynolda] have been from a third to a half more than I anticipated."

The aggrandizement of the house was in keeping with the growing prosperity of the Reynolds family, however. The R. J. Reynolds Tobacco Company experienced a sharp rise in profits after 1913, when it introduced Camel cigarettes, which soon became the best-selling brand in the world. Net profits of $2.9 million in 1912 climbed to $23.8 million by 1924. In 1922, the *Wall Street Journal* reported that the company's net earnings were the highest ever realized by a tobacco manufacturer.

Katharine Reynolds and Keen shared an insistence that all be done with "first class material and first class skill," as Keen's assistant, William Roy Wallace, recalled years later. Keen, for example, specified the most elaborate and costly method of painting for some of the main rooms. The process, known as French polishing, called for at least seven coats of white paint, each sanded or rubbed with pumice to a satin finish before the next application. The final coat was to be rubbed by hand to a uniform eggshell gloss.

The house's interior was far grander than the rather simple exterior. Each public room had its fine-carved marble fireplace mantel. In the living room, the reception hall, and the dining room were fluted pilasters with Corinthian, Doric, and Ionic capitals, as well as paneling, carved moldings, and rosettes. There were cast limestone walls and cornice in the reception hall, and the oak paneling in R. J.'s den featured book-matched

Cast limestone fluted pilaster and capital with
egg-and-dart carving in reception hall

Pennsylvania, furnished the floor tiles for the
front, side, and rear porches. In fact, Keen wrote
to Mercer to inquire about tiles but for unknown
reasons selected Enfield instead.

One of the most extraordinary interior ornamental features at Reynolda House was the decorative, hand-forged wrought-iron staircase railing
leading from the reception hall and around the
second-floor gallery. It was designed by the premier American maker of fine metalwork, Samuel
Yellin of Philadelphia. He championed the re-

Porch floor tile by Enfield Pottery & Tile Works,
Enfield, Pennsylvania

veneers and a beautifully carved shell-and-acan-
thus-leaf frieze.

Irving & Casson-A. H. Davenport, a famous
Boston furniture and woodworking firm, built and
installed the woodwork and cabinetry in the main
rooms on the first floor, including the organ case.
The firm also supplied fittings for the White
House and many of the period's finest residences.

Enfield Pottery & Tile Works, a Pennsylvania
firm on a par with Henry Chapman Mercer's more
famous Moravian Tile Works in Doylestown,

Wrought-iron gallery railing by
Samuel Yellin of Philadelphia

desk accessories, and a custom-made marble-top table.

For most of her furniture and carpets, and probably the curtains and accessories as well, Katharine Reynolds relied on selections from John Wanamaker, the famous Philadelphia department store. True to her thorough ways, she also obtained

vival of architectural wrought iron, inspired by the ironwork of medieval France, Germany, and Italy. Since he filled commissions for the best American architects of his day—including other Philadelphians besides Keen, such as Wilson Eyre, Will Price, and the firm of Walter Mellor and Arthur Meigs—his work was found in numerous American country houses.

Another fine supplier that contributed fittings to the house was E. F. Caldwell & Company of New York. The firm was associated with many outstanding buildings of the period, including Biltmore and Andrew Carnegie's Fifth Avenue mansion in New York, now the quarters of the Cooper-Hewitt Museum. It furnished the lighting fixtures and fireplace accessories, some choice

Wall lantern by E. F. Caldwell & Company,
lake porch

Photograph by Wes Stewart

estimates from W. & J. Sloane, a fancy home-furnishings specialist in New York.

Both stores were known for their full-service home-furnishings departments. Then at the zenith of its reputation, Wanamaker's provided a decorator, Edward A. Belmont, who came to Winston-Salem on several occasions to oversee installation of the home furnishings. Although Belmont's other contributions to the interiors cannot be documented from the available information, he most likely advised on the selection and arrangement of the furnishings and may well have contributed some designs for custom pieces.

In a letter to Belmont, Katharine wrote of a cabinet that was being built to house a Victrola.

Correspondence from Wanamaker's indicates that the store shipped more than two railroad carloads of merchandise. Three extant carpet floor plans from Wanamaker's indicate rug dimensions without, however, noting type or color of carpet to be put down.

While no itemized list of furniture from Wanamaker's has survived, the two Sloane's estimates were dutifully filed away by one of Katharine's secretaries. In the second estimate, less expensive items were substituted in almost

Breakfast room, c. 1918

every case for those first suggested. For example, two "richly carved" console sideboards for the dining room at $1,050 in the original estimate became two sideboards at $275 each in the second. The original dining table for $1,045 was scrapped and a smaller table for $290 substituted. Tapestry fabric at $20 a yard was changed to tapestry or English linen at $5 a yard. This clearly indicates that Katharine was economy-minded in her selection of furnishings. It may be imagined that she was successful in getting good prices from the Philadelphia store.

A room-by-room inventory taken in 1922 provides some clues about the furnishings, some of which are still in the house. For the most part, eighteenth-century revival styles dominated, which was fitting considering the Neoclassical wall decor. There were also a number of sixteenth- and seventeenth-century-style pieces.

The dining room, which still is furnished much as it was in Katharine's day, was in Adam Revival style. It featured an extension dining table, sixteen needlepoint-covered dining chairs, a pair of matching sideboards, and a pair of matching

Formal dining room, with Adam revival furniture, c. 1918

REYNOLDA HOUSE ARCHIVES

Marble fireplace mantel in dining room

Katharine's den must have been an elegant room, with its blue velvet carpet, blue-and-tan-striped silk sofa, and matching deep-arm easy chairs. A leather-topped parquetry desk placed in the center of the room attests to the fact that it was a working office.

From the description of the furnishings in the 1922 inventory, Katharine's bedroom was decorated in a French manner, with lace curtains and silk draperies in blue and champagne and a plum-colored rug. The double bed, covered with a champagne silk bedspread and bolster, was painted gray and blue and ornamented with carved flowers, and there were a matching dresser and dressing tables. Next to the bed were a pair of cabinets with hand-painted panels, and at its foot stood a blue-silk-covered chaise with pink satin pillows. The room also held a lady's roll-top desk, a pair of oval cabinets, several small bookcases, and a mahogany secretary.

THE ORGAN

Despite some apparent economies in furniture selection, the Reynolds family was more than willing to spend large sums on its house, as tellingly indicated by the thirty-thousand-dollar contract R. J. signed on January 27, 1917, with the Aeolian Company of New York for a pipe organ with four keyboards and a pedal footboard.

demilune cabinets, all in mahogany. The pieces were twentieth-century adaptations, rather than antiques or exact reproductions.

Two large, deep-tufted mauve velvet sofas, tapestry-covered armchairs, three large green carpets with foliate borders, and red-and-green-striped silk curtains gave the reception hall a rich, luxurious appearance.

The porches were furnished with wicker pieces and, in keeping with the style of the day, decorated with potted palms.

Long before the advent of high-fidelity systems and stereo speakers, large pipe organs powered by electricity were promoted as the equivalent of having a symphony orchestra in the home. Such instruments were capable of imitating the tones of woodwind, brass, string, and percussion instruments.

Aeolian's pipe organs were equipped with mechanisms that freed them from the clicks and rattles associated with organ playing in church. The rugs, tapestries, and curtains in a home absorbed harsh tones and helped produce a warmer, friendlier, and more mellow sound than can be imagined by someone who has heard an organ played only in churches and music halls.

While not so large as some organs by Aeolian, Reynolda's Number 1404 was a particularly fine example, boasting a sound that was majestic and strong. Although the company built at least 899 residential electric pipe organs between 1894 and 1932, the organ at Reynolda is one of the rare instruments still playable in its original location.

The organ was completed in January 1918 and

Console of Aeolian pipe organ by Irving & Casson-A. H. Davenport

Photograph by David Rolfe

The organ console is behind screen at left in reception hall.
The grill in ceiling at right covers the sound opening for the echo chamber.

left the factory in Garwood, New Jersey, in sixty-eight boxes weighing 2,245 pounds. It was placed on an Old Dominion steamship bound for Norfolk, Virginia. Then it traveled by rail to Winston-Salem, where it was installed at Reynolda shortly before Easter 1918.

The walnut organ console was placed near the dining room, where it still stands. The console was the visible portion of the musical system, but it was the 2,590 pipes in the chambers and attic that created the enormous sound at Reynolda. There were six openings in the walls and ceilings of the reception hall and the second-floor gallery, through which the sound poured into different locations in the hall. The main organ chamber (great, swell, pedal, and choir) and the antiphonal chamber provided immediacy. The echo chamber, located in the attic, filled the middle distance with sound through a grill located in the northwest corner of the ceiling.

Intriguingly, there is no evidence that the Reynoldses originally intended to install a pipe organ in their house. Surviving early plans dating from 1913 do not show any space devoted to

Pipes of the Aeolian organ

an organ. Precisely when and why it was decided to install an organ isn't known, but in a blueprint dating from January 1915, there is a small section labeled "organ" between the gallery and the loggia on the second floor. By 1916, the size of the proposed organ had greatly increased. Areas previously designated "gown room," "bedroom closet," and "linen closet" were now to accommodate organ pipes. A separate space was to house the antiphonal division, and, as noted above, a smaller area in the attic was marked out for the echo chamber.

The organ had an automatic-player mechanism. These mechanisms and the organ rolls played on them were keys to the popularity of the pipe organ in homes. With them, the instrument could make music even when there was no trained organist available to play. Organ rolls, like the piano rolls they resembled, were perforated paper rolls that passed over holes in a brass tracker bar. When a hole in the paper coincided with a hole in the tracker bar as the paper roll unwound by electric power, the note was played. Each musical selection required thousands of perforations. The longer and more complicated the music, the longer the roll and the more perforations on it.

In the Reynolda organ, the roll automatically supplied the notes, but the operator needed some degree of skill in order to add the tempo, stops, and expression from notations printed on the roll.

A later model, invented in 1917 and known as the Duo-Art Reproducing Organ, actually reproduced the original organist's playing style as well as the notes, and thus was a forerunner of recorded music. The company tried to interest Katharine Reynolds in the new mechanism, but she did not order it.

Aeolian included in its more than five thousand rolls both classical and popular musical selections, including operatic arias, symphonies, Bach's organ works, thirteen hundred hymns, and lighter fare. By the early 1920s, dance tunes and arrangements of popular songs from Broadway shows and radio broadcasts also were available.

The company kept tight control over its library of organ rolls. Only owners of an Aeolian pipe organ were permitted to buy a roll, and only one copy could be ordered. If the first copy was out of commission, it had to be returned before a replacement would be issued. Today, these paper-roll recordings, free of the scratches and hisses of old 78 rpm records, are one of the best ways to hear an early-twentieth-century musical performance.

There are approximately 250 organ rolls at Reynolda, some quite fragile but others in playable condition. The titles run the gamut from classical and sacred selections to "On the Road to Mandalay" and "Dear Old Pal of Mine."

Chapter 4

REYNOLDA IN FLOWER

1917-24

*K*atharine Reynolds had little time to think about her beautiful new house when it was finally ready for occupancy in December 1917. R. J. had been in the hospital since early fall.

"His trouble seems to have started [in the summer] with gastritis which went into a small stomach ulceration which healed very quickly, but left him in a rundown, nervous condition," Katharine wrote to a friend.

"Remedies" such as extracting all his teeth and keeping him in quarantine were tried. But since he had pancreatic cancer, deduced years later by forensic experts although not known by his doctors, these did little good.

"I am sorry to have to isolate Mr. Reynolds but worry in regard to his business was so definitely inhibiting his recovery that I felt he must have complete mental rest," his doctor wrote Katharine. "With your great knowledge of his business and his supreme confidence in your judgement [he] could not fail to keep his mind more or less active along business channels."

Katharine sensed that this was not going to help. "My dearest one," she wrote her husband in a letter that was saved but almost certainly never sent. "I am wondering if this strange separation, from one who loves you better than all others in the world is doing you good? . . . You will never know how terribly I miss you and love you and want your arms again around me and the children. . . . I'm looking forward and living for that day when we shall be together again in our once happy home."

Despite R. J.'s illness and her own poor health—probably caused by an undiagnosed childhood case of rheumatic fever that had left her with a weak heart—Katharine saw to it that Reynolda's facilities were used as she had intended. In the summer of 1917, she opened the dairy to local women and girls, who preserved forty-four thousand quarts of fruits and vegetables for a wartime food drive. Reynolda's gardens and greenhouses were the setting for a chrysanthemum show in October to raise money for the Red Cross. Also in October, Katharine accepted the chairmanship of the Woman's Liberty Loan Committee for North Carolina and arranged for the R. J. Reynolds Tobacco Company to subscribe a million dollars for liberty bonds for the war effort. In early December, she was even scheduled to speak to the Sorosis Club on Edgar Allen Poe; the talk was to be called "The Prince of American Literature."

That talk evidently was never delivered. She was with R. J. at Johns Hopkins Hospital in Baltimore just before Christmas when he rallied, and they made plans for him to come home in time for the holidays.

In Katharine's absence, Henrietta van den Berg supervised the move from Fifth Street to Reynolda

Henrietta van den Berg, or "Bum," the governess

REYNOLDA HOUSE ARCHIVES
Photograph by Matthews, Winston-Salem

in the second week of December. Van den Berg, a registered nurse, had come years earlier to help Katharine through a difficult pregnancy and had remained—affectionately nicknamed "Bum"—as governess and family confidante.

Bum detailed the tribulations of moving in letters to Katharine. "I saw Robert [Gibson, Reynolda's electrician] this morning and he will attend to the extension bell from Mr. Reynolds' room to your boudoir," she wrote on December 17.

"I know he [Mr. Reynolds] just can't but relax when he gets into his den. . . . I moved the furniture from [Room] 51 back to 44 yesterday, and have the Circasian [sic] Walnut Suite in 51. . . . I have done nothing as yet about the keys, except to lock the silver chest and linen room, and keep the keys in my pocket. . . . The ice cream freezer was connected up last Sunday, and it worked beautifully. The furnace is working well. The only thing we have not quite straightened out yet is the hot water. . . . It still turns muddy, or copper colored a few hours after it is done." The next day, she wrote, "I am thoroughly provoked that I have not yet heard a line from Mr. [Edward A.] Belmont. I am wiring him again today in your name and am going ahead as far as possible in placing things where I think they ought to go."

The children had been suffering from colds, and there were various other irritations. "I have not yet been able to give the help their lockers, as the carpenters are still working down there and it has been impossible to get things straight . . . ," Bum wrote. "They are having an awful time getting new lamps for the electric light fixtures. . . . The government has confiscated so many shipments that it seems impossible to do any better. . . . The boxes containing quilts, etc. from Wampoles, or McCutcheon's have not yet come. . . . No Chinese rugs have come either."

Despite these minor vexations, the Christmas decorations were in place and presents for the children and the staff purchased by the time Katharine and R. J. arrived at Reynolda a few days before Christmas. R. J. settled into his new den, now turned into a sickroom with a hospital bed and a nurse in attendance. Katharine resigned as president of the Woman's Liberty Loan Committee in January in order to be available to care for him. By February, he had recovered enough to go on a rabbit hunt, but he had lost seventy pounds since the summer and was far from healthy.

In May 1918, he was hospitalized again, this time at Thomas Jefferson Hospital in Philadelphia, where he remained until a little more than a week before his death in July. Katharine, who was often with him, had to attend to Reynolda's management from a distance. By mail, she engaged three teachers to staff the small elementary school she was planning to open on the grounds in the fall. But she wrote to Bum that she was "tired and discouraged" and to another correspondent that she had been "on [nursing] duty each night until 1 o'clock and frequently until 3."

The hospital ordeal came to an end eleven days before his death. On July 18, they started for home, R. J. on a cot in a private railroad car, accompanied by Katharine, a doctor, and two nurses. They arrived in Winston-Salem on July 20.

R. J. called for his attorney and orally amended

his will on July 23, leaving $120,000 to each of the two city hospitals, one for whites and one for blacks. He died on July 29, a day after his sixty-eighth birthday. The funeral service was held at Reynolda on the morning of July 31. As the casket was slowly wheeled out to the porte-cochere, an organist played "Nearer, My God, to Thee" on the organ R. J. had contracted for only a year and a half earlier.

A newspaper story of the time estimated the size of R. J.'s estate at ten million dollars. Katharine, of course, already owned Reynolda. As a mark of her husband's confidence in her judgment, he had named her (along with the Safe Deposit and Trust Company of Baltimore) executrix of his property. She received a third of R. J.'s wealth, which consisted of R. J. Reynolds Tobacco Company and other stock and real-estate holdings. The remainder was to be held in trust for their four children, now ages twelve, ten, eight, and six, until their twenty-eighth birthdays.

Katharine launched into widowhood with her accustomed energy. Immediately after the funeral, she had four large memorial scrapbooks of R. J.'s eulogies compiled—one for each of the children. When she had trouble sleeping late at night, she got up and went to the organ, where she solaced herself by quietly playing hymns and classical selections. On August 31, 1918, she announced that she would donate land for a new high school, to be known as R. J. Reynolds High School, and that she would pay for the construction of a three-thousand-seat school auditorium for the use of the community. Keen received the commission to design the school and auditorium, and Thomas Sears was selected as landscape architect.

Going out little during the winter of 1918–19, she continued to work on beautifying the landscape of Reynolda. She also made plans to expand the small school, which had opened in the fall of 1918 with three grades. Among its twenty pupils were Mary, Nancy, and Smith; Dick, who was twelve, was enrolled elsewhere. The other pupils included children in the neighborhood and the children of friends, relatives, and employees. Classes were held from nine in the morning to one in the afternoon in a cottage in Reynolda Village. The three teachers lived at Reynolda House. The two younger women shared the gentleman's guest room, and the school head occupied the lady's guest room.

Once they got over the immediate upset of their father's death, the children were able to enjoy the variety of activities among the friendly people who lived and worked on the estate. They had plenty of companions among their classmates and the children of the village. Still, they were the ones to whom the others looked up. When at home, Dick was a ringleader who liked to play jokes on his sisters and tease the teachers. The girls were "sweet and natural," in the words of one of the teachers. Smith, though quiet, was apt to come up with something clever to say during a lull in the conversation. The children enjoyed playing hide-and-seek in the organ chambers behind the tapestries on the second floor, and Nancy even learned to play the organ, although she never became adept. The automatic roll player spoiled her. "I couldn't play like that overnight, certainly not. . . . I could get so much more music out of a roll than I could get out of my hands," she said years later. Nancy would sit at the console, hidden behind a screen, pumping out organ rolls. After she amazed guests with her musical prowess, her mother would reveal the secret of her skill.

Years later, Nancy remembered her mother as something of a perfectionist who was determined that her children live up to a high standard. Nancy, who was nearsighted, thought she was not given glasses for a long time because her mother could not bear to admit that her daughter was less than perfect.

Yet Katharine was determined not to spoil the children. She insisted that they behave with respect toward servants. The girls took sewing lessons from a seamstress in Winston-Salem. They also had chores to perform. On Sunday nights—servants' night off—they served the meal that had been left for them in warming pans, and then they cleared the table and washed the dishes.

Their mother expected her children to do things for themselves.

R. J. must have shared her point of view, since one of the provisions in his will was that any money the children earned by their own efforts between their twenty-first and twenty-eighth birthdays would be doubled by his estate.

Dick had a·farm animal to care for, and the money he earned from its sale was to be treated as his spending money. He also worked in the tobacco factory for a few summers. The summer of 1920, he earned seventy cents a day at his job in the stemming room, the same as other operatives got. Later, he learned how to operate a cigarette machine. The summer he was sixteen, Dick worked a forty-five-hour week.

Mary and Nancy had a circle of cousins and school friends with whom they cooked fudge in the first-floor kitchen at Reynolda. They gave pajama parties and played dress-up in costumes and old evening gowns stored in the attic. Everyone at Reynolda, it seemed, loved costumes. Long before his marriage, R. J. had attended a costume party as one of the "fiddlers three" in the "Old King Cole" nursery rhyme. Katharine went to costume parties and gave lavish ones herself, including one for which she dressed up as Marie Antoinette, complete with strawberry blond wig.

One of the most elaborate costume events at Reynolda was not a party but a pageant. Pageants had been revived by English Arts and Crafts Movement proponents out of their fascination with the Middle Ages, when pageantry was associated with the church and royal entertainments. Progressive educators such as those running Reynolda School seized on pageants as an ideal form of learning that offered opportunities for bringing literature and history to life as well as teaching useful arts and crafts.

The Reynolda pageant, "Hiawatha, An Indian Passion Play," complete with costumes, dancing, and songs, was based on *The Song of Hiawatha* by Henry Wadsworth Longfellow. It was turned into a community project. "We used everybody on the place," recalled Ethel Sloan, a teacher and the director of the pageant.

The pageant took place outdoors at the edge of Lake Katharine on the evening of May 25, 1921. A professional orchestra provided the music, and a professor of dramatics at the University of North Carolina read portions of Longfellow's poem from a float anchored in the lake. Mary Reynolds—in black braided wig, buckskin dress, moccasins, and white stockings—played a starring role as Minnehaha. Nancy was a wind phantom. Smith's part, if any, isn't known, but he may have been the instigator of the whole idea. In a diary entry on January 24, 1921, Mary wrote that "Smith has an idea for an Indian play. We worked on it all afternoon. I have been working on a song in a make-believe Indian language."

The importance that Katharine attached to the pageant, described in the ever-adulatory *Sentinel* as "one of the most beautiful outdoor events in the history of Winston-Salem," is conveyed by the imposing, oversize, leather-bound commemorative photo albums she had produced.

By 1921, R. J.'s death had receded into the background and Reynolda was in full flower. The farm was flourishing, and Katharine's prize herd of 110

"Hiawatha, An Indian Passion Play," presented by Reynolda School and the community, with Bowman Gray, Jr., as Hiawatha and Mary Reynolds as Minnehaha, May 25, 1921

"Hiawatha, An Indian
Passion Play," presented
on the shore of Lake Katharine,
May 25, 1921

REYNOLDA HOUSE ARCHIVES
Photograph by Holladay

Nancy Reynolds in profile,
center, with other Wind
Phantoms during "Hiawatha,
An Indian Passion Play,"
May 25, 1921

REYNOLDA HOUSE ARCHIVES
Photograph by Holladay

purebred Jersey cows took 142 ribbons at fairs in North Carolina, South Carolina, Virginia, and Georgia. The prize bull, Raleigh's Noble Boy, purchased in 1920 for two thousand dollars, took the grand prize at five fairs.

The school, now expanded to seven grades for about 150 pupils, was going well, too. The facilities Katharine had planned back in 1919 included a swimming pool, four garden rooms, a motion-picture machine, a fully equipped shop for the boys, and a model home where the girls could be drilled in "the duties required of the average woman in the home . . . cooking, sewing, house cleaning, bedmaking, washing, ironing," as the *Winston-Salem Journal* reported on August 31, 1919.

This rather grandiose scheme was not, in fact, carried out. Reynolda School was conducted in a Keen-designed building known as "the tempo-

Prize bull Xenias Rower, Jr., held by Smith Reynolds, with Albert Wharton, son of Reynolda's superintendent, in rear, Maryland Fair, 1925

REYNOLDA HOUSE ARCHIVES
Photograph from the shop of Robert F. Hildebrand, New York City.

rary schoolhouse." It served as the main schoolhouse for the remainder of the school's existence, through 1923. After the school closed, the structure was turned into Reynolda's administration building.

To run her enlarged school, Katharine had hired a new principal in the late spring of 1919. He was J. Edward Johnston (1893–1951), a handsome twenty-six-year-old just back from war service. Johnston had graduated from Davidson College in Davidson, North Carolina, in 1914 and then was a school principal in Washington, North Carolina, for a brief period. He served overseas during World War I as a lieutenant with the Fifth Field Artillery Battalion, First Division, under General Pershing. He and several of the teachers he hired started their Reynolda careers by taking summer-school classes at Columbia University's teachers' college, at Katharine's expense.

Reynolda School, with Nancy in group at left and J. Edward Johnston, principal, at right, c. 1919

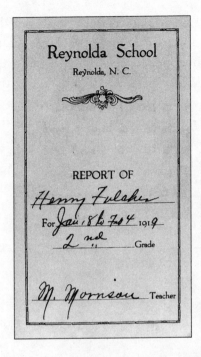

Reynolda School

Reynolda, N. C.

REPORT OF

Henry Fulcher

For *Jan. 18 to Feb 4* 1919

2 nd Grade

M. Mornson Teacher

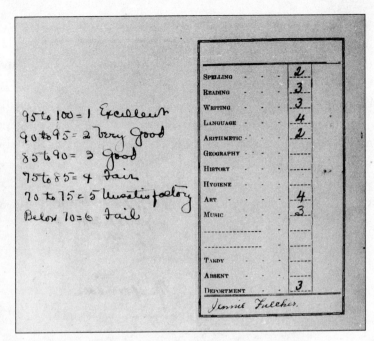

95 to 100 = 1 Excellent
90 to 95 = 2 Very Good
85 to 90 = 3 Good
75 to 85 = 4 Fair
70 to 75 = 5 Unsatisfactory
Below 70 = 6 Fail

SPELLING		2
READING		3
WRITING		3
LANGUAGE		4
ARITHMETIC		2
GEOGRAPHY		-----
HISTORY		-----
HYGIENE		-----
ART		4
MUSIC		3
-------------		-----
-------------		-----
TARDY		
ABSENT		
DEPORTMENT		3

Jennie Fulcher.

Reynolda School report card of Henry Fulcher, the night watchman's son, 1919

REYNOLDA HOUSE ARCHIVES

Copy prpint made from materials loaned by Bynum Fulcher

By all accounts, Reynolda School offered a progressive education well ahead of its time. Subjects such as French, art, music, and physical education were taught by specialists who could order whatever books and supplies they wanted. The whole of the estate was the children's laboratory. They also were taken on trips—for example, they saw the state legislature in session at Raleigh. Although tuition costs are not known, the school was not free. Katharine also received an allowance from the county for some of the children who attended the school, Nancy Reynolds later recalled.

The staff of eight teachers at first boarded in town and came out to Reynolda each morning by bus. But on January 16, 1921, they moved into

The manse, used first as a
residence for teachers at
Reynolda School

REYNOLDA HOUSE ARCHIVES

Reynolda School bus,
driven by Buck Wharton,
c. 1919–23

REYNOLDA HOUSE ARCHIVES

the "teacherage," as one of them called the manse next door to Reynolda Presbyterian Church. The minister lived in another house on the property at the time. Alma Mitchell, one of the teachers, later recalled that "the same Philadelphia decorator [Edward A. Belmont] who did her [Katharine's] house decorated the teacherage."

Working and living at Reynolda was a perpetual house party for the teachers, who were given the run of the estate. On snowy winter days and evenings, they had marshmallow roasts in one of the huge fireplaces at Reynolda House. Sundays, Katharine invited them in turns to dinner. With a bit of hyperbole, one of the teachers described the "sumptuous meals, with course after course and four or five butlers hovering over us with delicious food." Some nights, the rugs in the reception hall were rolled back and dance-music organ rolls were put on. "We did the Two-Step, the Waltz, the Cheek-to-Cheek, the Bunny Hug, and the Paul Jones," recalled Alma Mitchell. "We sometimes danced until one or two o'clock and got up and taught school at nine the next morning." Katharine also enjoyed the dancing, Ed Johnston frequently serving as her partner.

About two weeks after the Hiawatha pageant, on June 7, 1921, approximately eight hundred guests enjoyed a concert by the new Metropolitan Opera tenor, Mario Archer Chamlee. The party had to be moved indoors hurriedly because of rain. More important, the occasion was an unannounced prenuptial celebration for the wedding of Katharine Reynolds and Edward Johnston. Although she might have revealed her news to family members and close friends at dinner that evening, no public announcement of the impending wedding was made.

Mary Reynolds, age twelve, confided to her diary on June 11, "At about 7:15 Mother was married to Mr. Johnston. The affair was very quiet. Smith was ring barrier [sic] and Nancy and myself were flower girls. We are trying to keep it quiet but about the hole [sic] town knows it."

Attended only by their immediate families and several of Katharine's close friends, the couple was married by D. Clay Lilly, Katharine's former minister and a longtime family friend. The ceremony took place in front of the marble fireplace in Reynolda's reception hall. Katharine walked down the stairs to the great, swelling chords of Mendelssohn's wedding march, played on the organ. Subsequently, her daughters and granddaughters who were married at home did the same.

Nobody from R. J.'s side of the family, including his brother Will, who was now president of the R. J. Reynolds Tobacco Company, appears to have been at the wedding. The girls and Smith served as attendants, but Dick was probably still at boarding school and was not present.

Katharine Reynolds and J. Edward Johnston

On their wedding day, Edward Johnston was twenty-eight to Katharine's forty-one. A graceful, charming, and handsome young man, he made friends easily. He had grown up in Florence, South Carolina. Ed's father had died when he was four years old, but his mother, Lola Johnston, moved to Winston-Salem and lived in a house in Reynolda Park designed for her by Keen and paid for by Katharine. She became a pillar of local society.

Years later, one of the teachers at Reynolda School recalled that "Mrs. Reynolds and Edward Johnston carried on a speedy courtship, and we [teachers] stood on the sidelines and watched. She was thirteen years older than Edward. . . . We all wondered who did the proposing." The couple appeared to be devoted to each other. "They were two lovebirds," recalled Elizabeth Wade, one of the servants.

A younger man who married a rich older woman was bound to attract attention. The wedding was a nine days' wonder in Winston-Salem. Emma Bernard Kaminer, a college chum of Katharine's who was one of the few individuals outside the immediate family to be present, caught her friend up on the gossip in several letters to Katharine in London on her two-month Euro-

pean honeymoon. Two boys who "peeked in a window" during the ceremony had spread the word of the wedding, and townspeople had come out to Reynolda to "see what they could see. It must be gratifying and inspiring too to have the people of your home so interested in your affairs," Emma wrote, "for if they didn't like you they wouldn't care a damn when you married or what or where!"

Interest in the wedding extended to Emma's hometown of Asheville, North Carolina, 150 miles from Winston-Salem. "A woman at the club here asked me if it was true that you were forty-eight and Edward twenty-two. . . . Another told me that she thought it was fine for you to marry the man who was at the head of the R. J. Reynolds Tobacco Co., and that you'd made over all of your property to him," Emma wrote in another letter. Katharine apparently was amused by the two letters, because she saved them.

On their return to Winston-Salem, Ed and Katharine were received with rounds of parties in their honor. Regardless of the warm welcome, in the fall of 1921, they decided to close Reynolda House for a while and move the family to New York. Accompanied by Bum and a nursemaid, as well as an entourage of turtles, lovebirds, and Smith's pet monkey, they took an apartment on the upper East Side and enrolled Mary, Nancy, and Smith in private school. Dick was in boarding school in Baltimore.

J. Edward Johnston in sun porch, c. 1921

Katharine in sun porch, c. 1921

Ed took a bank training course at the Guaranty Trust Company in New York that would be necessary for his new position as a trust officer at Wachovia Bank. By the winter of 1921, Katharine must have known that she was expecting a child. At her age and with her history of difficult pregnancies, it was wise to put herself under the care of a New York specialist.

On May 1, 1922, a daughter was born to Katharine two or three months premature; the child lived for only a day. It was a tragic end to the family's sojourn in New York.

By June, they all returned to Winston-Salem and Reynolda, where they picked up the strands of their lives. Now, the social activities of Dick, Mary, and Nancy were followed closely in the society columns.

Katharine resumed her role as one of Winston-Salem's most indefatigable organizers. She was elected to the board of managers of the Juvenile Relief Association, attended meetings of the Embroidery Club and the Whist Club, and was working with Keen on a clubhouse overlooking the outdoor swimming pool; the clubhouse was never built. Ed, now at Wachovia Bank as an assistant trust officer, was elected chief elder of Reynolda Presbyterian Church.

In January 1923, Katharine held a meeting for forty friends to organize an auxiliary to the Juvenile Relief Association and to apply for membership in the Association of Junior Leagues of America. The group became the first Junior League in the state and the forty-sixth nationally. On March 31, she announced the closing of Reynolda School at the end of the school year. Mary was already away at boarding school, and Nancy, who would finish seventh grade in June, was to attend the new R. J. Reynolds High School in the fall. The Reynolda School building was needed for office space. Katharine had also hired her old friend Dr. Lilly as minister of Reynolda Presbyterian Church. The terms of his contract called for him to occupy the "teacherage."

By the spring of 1923, there was a new enthusiasm at Reynolda: polo. A school athletic field was turned into a polo field. Ed was elected president of the polo team, the third in the state. His team members included Fred Hanes, James G. Hanes, Robert Hanes, Reynolda superintendent Clint Wharton, and Charles Barton Keen. The architect and his family had recently moved into the Hotel Robert E. Lee downtown with the announced intention of settling in Winston-Salem; they did not stay, however, but returned to Philadelphia less than a year later.

The first match, on June 15, was a benefit for the Juvenile Relief Home. People came from as far as Charlotte and Greensboro to see Ed's team win 5–3, thanks in part to his two goals.

The Johnstons were in a social whirl in 1923, frequently giving parties at Reynolda, such as a dinner for forty in honor of the marriage of Dewitt

Mary and Nancy Reynolds on steps of lake porch, c. 1921

REYNOLDA HOUSE ARCHIVES
Photograph by Matthew, Winston-Salem

Chatham and Ralph G. Hanes. On July 6, they gave a garden party for twelve hundred guests to welcome Keen and his wife and Dr. Lilly to town. David H. Blair, commissioner of the Internal Revenue Service, and his wife also were honorees at the party. Punch was served in bowls made from blocks of ice in which roses were embedded, and each garden parterre had an assigned host and hostess. The refreshments were brought from New York in a refrigerated railroad car, and the Paul Whiteman Orchestra, also from New York, played. On November 15, there was a masquerade ball in honor of May Coan and Kenneth Mountcastle, who were to be married two days later. Costumed guests danced in the reception hall to the strains of a New York orchestra. The "lake porch warmly aglow with its glorious fire" was a scene of "almost medieval grandeur," according to a newspaper account describing the event.

The parties continued through Christmas. On December 1, for example, there was a buffet supper for 125 (dressed eggs, caviar on toast, sardines, chicken salad sandwiches, cream cheese and nut bread, turkey hash in patty cases, sliced ham, fruit salad, rolls, potato chips, molasses tarts). The next day, Katharine gave a buffet for her head gardener, Robert Conrad, and his bride.

The Winston-Salem polo team, September 9, 1923. From left to right are A. C. Wharton, Carl Ogburn, W. V. Slocock, James G. Hanes, Benjamin F. Bernard, Watt Martin, Thurmond Chatham, J. Edward Johnston, and Fred M. Hanes.

REYNOLDA HOUSE ARCHIVES
Photograph by Matthews, Winston-Salem

By January 1924, an air of quiet descended. Katharine resigned from some of her public activities. At forty-three, she was pregnant again and restricting her projects. She had told friends that she would give her husband a child even if it killed her, and in March, she moved to New York to be near her doctors. Ed arrived in New York from Winston-Salem on May 10, two days after R. J. Reynolds Auditorium was dedicated. Ten days later, on May 20, Katharine gave birth to Edward Johnston, Jr. The baby was fine and, for a few days, so was the mother, but on May 23, she died of an embolism. Today, she might have survived. Her weak heart and the enforced months of bed rest then deemed essential for "delicate" women during and after pregnancy probably contributed to the blockage that took her life.

Dick, Nancy, and Smith were at Reynolda when they learned of their mother's death. Mary was at school in Bryn Mawr, Pennsylvania. At the train station in Philadelphia, she got on the special train carrying Katharine's body, Ed, and the new baby.

In Winston-Salem, stores and businesses closed on the day of Katharine's funeral. Two services took place, one at Reynolda for relatives, friends, and employees and the other at the new R. J. Reynolds Auditorium, where delegations from most of the city's organizations paid their respects to "the woman who has perhaps done more for this city than any other woman who has ever lived here," in the words of a writer for the *Journal* on May 26. Among those attending the private funeral was Charles H. Babcock of New York, the future husband of Mary Reynolds. He had been a colleague of Ed's at Guaranty Trust in New York and had stayed friendly with the family. Katharine's casket, draped with a blanket of orchids, sat in state in Reynolda's reception hall before the funeral service, conducted jointly by Dr. Lilly and the Reverend Neal Anderson. During the service, as reported by the *Journal* on May 29, Charles G. Vardell "touched the keys of the organ and the sweet strains swept gently throughout the home," as once again the instrument marked a solemn occasion at Reynolda House. The procession to Salem Cemetery consisted of those who attended both funerals, making it "one of the greatest that ever flowed from this city on such a mission bent." Katharine was buried in the family plot next to R. J.

"And so we were orphans," recalled Nancy Reynolds years later. Their parents had died within six years of each other, leaving them a legacy of money and a great country estate. Powerful as these were, they would not be enough to protect them from the encroachments of the world.

Chapter 5

DRIFTING

1924-34

A great country estate tends to survive many generations in countries such as England, where the eldest son usually inherits the property, along with the fortune required to care for it. In the United States, where the estate and the money usually are divided among all the heirs, the owner's death puts the property in jeopardy and in practical terms often leads to its dismantling.

The cost of maintenance turned many large early-twentieth-century American country houses into white elephants, too big to live in and too costly to keep up. The growth of the suburbs also contributed to the demise of such properties, since it became far more profitable to tear down a large house and subdivide the land than to keep things as they were.

If maintaining the property did not bankrupt the family or interfere with its opportunity to prosper on the old estate, then the American penchant of every generation to reinvent itself did. Frequently, the second generation had no interest in the old family place. In general, by the late 1930s, running a self-sufficient community such as Reynolda was no longer regarded by wealthy scions as a highly desirable pastime.

Partly because the heirs did not need to sell and partly because Katharine's will made it clear that she wanted them to hold onto it, Reynolda was not dismantled. The will directed that the

Aerial view of Reynolda looking west, c. 1927. On an axis from bottom center to top center are the post office, the trough at the intersection of the village entrance and Reynolda Road, Reynolda Presbyterian Church, the Katharine Johnston Memorial Building, and the Katharine Johnston Memorial. On the cross axis from left to right are the superintendent's house, the plumber's house, the church, the manse, the secretary's house, and, behind it, the electrician's house. The poultry runs are at far right.

core of the estate—house, recreational grounds, formal gardens, and village with its outbuildings—was to be held in trust for her children and second husband until the youngest child was twenty-one.

The staff members continued to do their jobs, under the supervision of a property manager hired by the Safe Deposit and Trust Company of Baltimore, which had been overseeing the management of the family fortune ever since R. J. selected it to manage his estate. There was, however, a loss of momentum without Katharine's leadership. Among the first signs of retrenchment was the dispersal of her prize herd of Jersey cattle, sold at auction in 1926. Farm operations grew increasingly slack. The dairy cows gave less and less milk. Hams hung in the smokehouse, but they were often hard and tough.

Reynolda, like all great country places, took a lot of money to run. The average annual expenditure over and above any income realized was $47,687, as a summary of operations between 1922 and 1930 indicates.

A number of financial resources were available to make up the deficit. They included dividends from and sales of the common stock that was part of Katharine's estate and assessments on the trust funds of the Reynolds children. Each child had inherited substantial blocks of Reynolds stock, which grew increasingly valuable as the company prospered. By 1931, the R. J. Reynolds Tobacco Company, now run by a group that included R. J.'s younger brother Will, who was chairman of the board, became the most profitable tobacco company in the United States, with annual sales of three hundred million dollars, according to *Fortune* magazine.

Another source of capital for running Reynolda came from the sale of some of its land. Katharine herself began this practice in the 1920s when she created a subdivision known in her time as Reynolda Park, which was laid out by Thomas Sears, her landscape architect. Later, Charles Barton Keen designed some of the houses that went up on the lots. In 1925, an 83.6-acre parcel was sold to Bowman Gray. Gray, then the president of the R. J. Reynolds Tobacco Company, had a Norman Revival mansion designed by local architect Luther Lashmit and retained Sears to landscape the property, known as Graylyn.

Reynolda Farm realized some earnings from the sale of products such as milk, hay, vegetables, poultry, and honey. The quarry still produced stone, and the landscaping and plumbing departments took on private jobs for profit. Cut flowers and plants were sold out of the greenhouses, and the estate's bus service netted a few hundred dollars some years. The profits generated by all these departments were small, but they did help defray some of the cost of their own existence.

REYNOLDA BUS SCHEDULE

FARE

Straight through fare 15c or 2 tokens for 25c.

Straight midway (Calvin Wiley School) 7c or 4 tokens for 25c.

ROUTE

Reynolda to Arbor Road, to Oaklawn Ave., to Buena Vista Road, to Virginia Road, to N. Hawthorne Road, to Glade St., to West End Boulevard, to N. Spruce St., to 5th St., to Main St. (Court House.) RETURNING: Third St., to Cherry St., to 5th St., to N. Spruce Street thence by above route to Reynolda.

BUS STOPS ON NEAR SIDE OF INTERSECTIONS

EFFECTIVE JUNE 1ST. 1929
(SUBJECT TO CHANGE WITHOUT NOTICE)

OVER

REYNOLDA BUS SCHEDULE

WEEK-DAY SCHEDULE

Lv. Reynolda	Lv. Court House
6:20 A. M.	6:40 A. M.
7:00	7:30
8:00	8:30
9:00	9:30
10:00	10:30
11:00	11:30
12:00 Noon	12:30 P. M.
1:00 P. M.	1:30
2:00	2:30
3:00	3:30
4:00	4:30
5:00	5:30
6:00	6:30
7:00	7:30
8:00	8:30
9:00	9:30
10:30	11:00

SUNDAYS AND HOLIDAYS*

7:00 A. M.	7:30
9:00	9:30
10:00	10:30
12:30 P. M.	1:00 P. M.
4:00	4:30
6:30	7:00
8:30	9:00

*Christmas and Easter Monday

EFFECTIVE JUNE 1ST. 1929
(SUBJECT TO CHANGE WITHOUT NOTICE)

OVER

Bus schedule, 1929

REYNOLDA HOUSE ARCHIVES
From materials loaned by Bynum Fulcher

Despite the various enterprises and the comfortable cushion of tobacco stock, running Reynolda at full tilt must have seemed fiscally irresponsible to the bank officers charged with overseeing the family fortune. This became especially true as the children grew older and spent less and less time there.

In 1930, Stewart Warnken, the farm manager hired by the bank, drew up a list of assets and liabilities with a view to shutting down operations and leasing out Reynolda House. "If an orderly disposal of the assets could be had, under proper conditions, they should produce in many instances 25% to 50% more than the values placed thereon," Warnken wrote in a statement of assets dated May 1, 1930. Whether out of concern for employees, lack of a suitable tenant, the realization that upkeep would still cost money, a desire to preserve something that Katharine had built and loved, the fact that she had clearly wished for the property to be retained, or a combination of these considerations, nothing was done about Warnken's proposal.

In the weeks after Katharine's death in May 1924, it is doubtful that anyone in the family was thinking of Reynolda's upkeep or future. The more important question of how to care for the four children must have loomed large in the minds of their guardians, Will Reynolds and Ed Johnston.

It was decided that the summer tour of Europe planned by their mother should go forward. Accompanied by cousins, friends, their old governess Bum (Henrietta van den Berg), and their mother's former secretary and friend Ben Bernard, all four Reynolds children boarded a steamship for England and prepared to make their first grand tour.

When they returned home in September, Dick, eighteen, enrolled at North Carolina Agricultural and Engineering College (later North Carolina State University) in Raleigh. Mary, sixteen, returned to Miss Wright's boarding school in Bryn Mawr. Nancy, fourteen, went to R. J. Reynolds High School for two years. Smith, thirteen, went off to Woodberry Forest School in Virginia. By 1926, Nancy also was away at school, and Reynolda House was empty except for holidays and summers, only a housekeeper and a few servants to care for it.

Ed Johnston observed the customary year of mourning for his late wife, giving up his beloved polo and supervising the construction of a memorial obelisk and a large Sunday-school building at Reynolda Presbyterian Church. He, too, soon moved out of Reynolda, joining his mother, Lola Johnston, and his infant son in the house that Katharine had commissioned Keen to design for her mother-in-law. Johnston remarried in Baltimore in 1928 and was no longer in close contact with the Reynolds family. He died in Baltimore in 1951.

R. J. Reynolds had created the kind of wealth that made the prospect of earning a living unnecessary for his children, although they would not gain full control of their inheritance until they were twenty-eight. Uncle Will maintained tight control over the purse strings but allowed Mary and Nancy to enjoy world travel. In the spring of 1927, Mary was eighteen and had graduated from Miss Wright's. Nancy, sixteen, had completed her year at Rosemary Hall in Greenwich, Connecticut, and been accepted to Agnes Scott College. They arranged to take their second trip to Europe that summer. "We want to sell our cars here and buy new ones over there. We may not come back to school, it depends," Nancy confided to her diary. She returned in the fall of 1927 for a few months, while Mary stayed in Paris to attend art school. In the winter of 1928, accompanied by a chaperon hired by Uncle Will, the two sisters cruised the Mediterranean and traveled down the Nile, visiting such places as Madeira, Algeria, Egypt, Jerusalem, Nazareth, Beirut, Damascus, Budapest, and Vienna. They returned to Winston-Salem periodically. For example, they came back in the summer of 1928, when their schedule included golf, horseback riding, French lessons, weekends at Roaring Gap, and time for falling in and out of love.

At their age, their mother had been training to become a teacher. For the rest of her life, Katharine had held education as one of her most cherished values. So it is easy to imagine that if she had lived, she would have expected her children to complete a college education. Uncle Will's attitude—common at the time—was that girls who were going to get married didn't need college. In 1928, the sisters enrolled for the fall semester at Columbia University's general-studies division, but mainly they traveled and had a good time.

All this, of course, was exactly as it was supposed to be in an era when the proper "work" of affluent young women was to acquire polish and social skills and ultimately make a good marriage. By 1930, both sisters married suitable young men. Almost back-to-back weddings were held at Reynolda on December 16, 1929, for Mary and on January 6, 1930, for Nancy. Dick escorted each of his sisters down the aisle.

Mary, twenty-one, married Charles H. Babcock, who had been brought up in Indiana and had graduated from the Wharton School at the University of Pennsylvania. Just as at her mother's wedding to Ed Johnston, the ceremony, held in front of the fireplace, was performed by D. Clay Lilly; Charles G. Vardell played the organ. Nancy, twenty, married Henry Bagley, an Atlantan working in advertising at Condé Nast in New York. The Babcocks moved to Philadelphia, where Charlie Babcock had a job at Guaranty Trust. Nancy and Henry Bagley set up housekeeping in a New York apartment.

Higher education held no more appeal for Dick and Smith than it did for their sisters. Dick dropped out of college after a year or so and moved to New York, while Smith declined to enroll at all. Uncle Will was not at all delighted when his nephews decided, several years apart, to enter the exciting new field of aviation by purchasing their own planes.

Dick and Smith may have learned to fly at one of the two early airfields in Winston-Salem. Such fields all around the country attracted weekend crowds, who came to see stunt flyers perform and to risk taking a ride. The first local airfield to open, in December 1919, was Maynard Field, on a thirty-five-acre piece of land between Winston-Salem and the town of Kernersville. Charles Field opened nearby in 1922. Mary also was bitten by

The wedding of Nancy Reynolds and Henry Bagley, January 6, 1930

the aviation bug and took flying lessons, according to Nancy Reynolds's recollections.

Years later, residents remembered Dick's executing barrel rolls and loops in the sky above Reynolda before landing on the lawn. He received one of the first licenses issued to an American citizen by the Fédération Aeronautique Internationale, signed by its secretary at the time, Orville Wright.

Dick Reynolds, who died in December 1964 at the age of fifty-eight, pursued many activities during his somewhat short and exciting life, including a brief stint as mayor of Winston-Salem in 1941–42. He left office after a year to enlist in the navy. As navigator of the USS *Makin Island*, he led the Seventh Fleet into the Lingayén Gulf. He returned home with the rank of lieutenant commander and a Bronze Star for heroism.

These war exploits were in the future when Dick began his first business venture. He founded Reynolds Aviation, a small business that operated from several airfields, including Miller Field, Winston-Salem's first real airport. At the opening-day festivities for the airport on September 8, 1928, his brother, Smith, age seventeen, won the amateur air race.

Nancy Reynolds and Alfred Drage, the son of Reynolda's horticulturist, recalled later that Smith took flying lessons in Winston-Salem from Mac McGinnis, who started Camel City Airlines, forerunner of Piedmont Airlines. Like his brother, Smith earned a license signed by Orville Wright. He also became adept as an aviation mechanic.

In 1930, at age nineteen, Smith flew across the continental United States from New York to Los Angeles in an unofficial record time of twenty-eight hours and three minutes. In 1931–32, he completed another glorious escapade by flying from London to Hong Kong alone in a tiny Savoia Marchetti amphibian plane. The 128-day trip, detailed in a log that Nancy Reynolds had privately printed after Smith's death, was filled with mechanical challenges and adventures in the places Smith landed. His sense of humor about

himself and his life shows clearly in a letter he wrote to his aunt Maxie from Hanoi in March 1932, toward the end of his trip: "So far, except for Smith trouble, motor trouble, plane trouble, the trip has been just lovely. If I didn't have ambitions of becoming a certified public accountant, I think that I would not come home. . . . My Hindu Sadhu man told me that I would receive 27,243 rupees (money) in October so I guess I had best return."

Although he died before the age of twenty-one, Smith was married twice, the first time at age eighteen. After being divorced from his first wife, Anne Cannon, who bore him a daughter, he married Broadway torch singer Libby Holman on November 29, 1931. The ceremony was performed by a justice of the peace in Monroe, Michigan, one of the few places in the United States where legal minors could marry without the consent of parents or guardians.

Smith and Libby did not publicly announce their marriage until after his solo trip to Hong Kong. They arrived at Reynolda on June 5, 1932, with the announced intention of staying for at least a year. They settled into the master suite. Smith and Libby appear to have started by enjoying Reynolda to the utmost—swimming, playing tennis, riding, and lazing by the outdoor swimming pool. While she sang and took piano lessons from Charles G. Vardell, he saw to the

Smith Reynolds in front of his Ford 5-AT (air transport) Tri-Motor

repair of his plane, made plans for another flight, and was tutored in mathematics.

The Reynolda staff liked Libby, according to the reminiscences of Nadeina Gibson Buchanan. Libby took the trouble to "actually go down to the kitchen [in the basement] and tell Mattie [the cook], 'Oh, that was such a good meal. I appreciate that,'" Buchanan recalled many years later.

Smith and Libby gave house parties featuring swimming, canoeing, barbecues, and free-flowing whiskey. Their guests were an oddly assorted group of her actor friends—such as Beatrice Lillie, Clifton Webb, Spring Byington, and Blanche Yurka—and the Winston-Salem companions of his boyhood.

On the night of July 5, after a small party at the lake, a shot was heard around eleven-thirty. Smith was found in the house with a bullet wound in his temple. Libby and Smith's friend and secretary, Ab Walker, drove him to the hospital, where he died without regaining consciousness.

After Smith's death, Libby testified that she could not remember the events of the day and evening of her husband's death. Ab Walker changed his account of his movements several times, after first declaring that he would "take to the grave" the story of what had happened that night. Their accounts drew suspicion, and they were indicted by a grand jury for Smith's murder.

The story was made to order for the tabloids.

Newspapers from around the country sent their most dexterous writers to report on developments. These included the news that Libby was pregnant as well as speculation about wild parties, heavy drinking, and a possible romance between Libby and Ab Walker. An unrelenting barrage of negative publicity rained down on Smith's family, who had gathered in Winston-Salem.

The family decided that there was not enough evidence to determine beyond a reasonable doubt what had happened, and that the only outcome of a public trial would be more sensationalism. Shortly before the trials of Libby Holman and Ab Walker were to start, Will Reynolds wrote to the prosecutor, Carlyle Higgins, sent a copy of the letter to the presiding judge, and released the contents publicly. He requested that the cases be dropped "because of some doubt in my mind and in the minds of Smith's brother and sisters. . . . I realize that the cases are now entirely a matter between the state and the accused and that Smith's family are not a party to the proceedings. I trust, however, that your high sense of public duty will enable you, after careful consideration, to request that the cases be given the direction indicated."

The letter accomplished its purpose. Within a few weeks, Higgins announced that the state of North Carolina would not go forward with the cases. In later years, Higgins was one of the few individuals connected with the case ever to discuss it publicly. He stated that there was not enough evidence for a conviction and affirmed his belief that Libby Holman had not been responsible for Smith's death.

Since Smith had been a minor, there were many legal questions about his will. Eventually, a settlement was worked out that led to the establishment by Smith's brother and sisters of the Z. Smith Reynolds Foundation. The foundation, incorporated in 1936 with assets of $7.2 million from Smith's estate, has donated more than $231 million to educational and charitable organizations in every county in North Carolina.

Smith's death cast a pall over Reynolda for many years. Indeed, even today, it retains a haunting power to fascinate, perhaps because the facts will never be resolved. It would not have been surprising if Smith's death had led to the closing or sale of Reynolda. But this did not happen. With the hindsight of more than six decades, it can be seen that the tragic incident did not displace Reynolda from the affections of the family. It did, however, cause them to go to great lengths to avoid further publicity. When Dick Reynolds married Elizabeth "Blitz" McCaw Dillard of Winston-Salem on January 1, 1933, the wedding was a quieter affair than those of his two sisters several years earlier.

After their wedding trip, Dick and his wife returned to Winston-Salem and lived at Reynolda for about two years, during which they started work on their own country estate at Devotion, North Carolina, a few miles down the mountain from Roaring Gap.

In 1935, the cost of maintaining the property prompted a recommendation from the estate's trustees that Reynolda be offered for sale. The family members met; at first, it looked as though none wanted the property. Then Mary and Charlie Babcock stepped forward and made an offer to buy out the interests of the other heirs, thereby becoming the new owners of the estate. Signifying the change of ownership, Reynolda's balance sheet for the year shows that a purchase contract was drawn up with a note of $250,000, payable August 8, 1936. The same document records a payment of $53,000 to the corporation from the Babcocks at the beginning of the year for Reynolda's maintenance, as well as a payment of $15,000 for the bungalow furnishings. A new chapter in Reynolda's history was about to begin.

Chapter 6

THE BABCOCK ERA

1935-36

The Babcocks' acquisition of Reynolda ensured the survival of its way of life for at least the immediate future, which delighted the Reynolda Villagers. The renovations and land improvements the Babcocks soon undertook gave additional work to those on the estate. Even before the house was renovated, Charlie Babcock took steps to streamline farm operations and to reduce the annual operating deficit, which by 1934 had risen to about sixty-seven thousand dollars.

At the end of 1935, in what was clearly his first report to the new owners, Stewart Warnken noted that "the entire property presents a much better appearance than it has for the past ten or twelve years, and the morale of the organization has been improved considerably due to the removal of the uncertainty of the future that previously existed."

Warnken enumerated some of the steps that had been taken. The commercial landscape department had billed $19,390 worth of work, with a net profit of $2,370, compared to a profit of only $900 the previous year. "The outlook for this work is promising as a number of jobs in the medium cost field were obtained during the past year." The plumbing and heating department realized a profit of $2,475, compared to a loss of $1,100 the year before. The greenhouse, while not operating at a profit, had taken on more design work and was selling table and wedding decorations, corsages, window boxes, terrariums, and cemetery decorations. The annuals and perennials grown in the greenhouses were being sold to the public. Farming operations showed a loss, but hay was being sold at current market prices, and "an effort was made during the past year to eliminate surplus equipment and livestock and replace with modern equipment and sound mules."

The Babcocks continued the old policy of transferring some acreage to new uses. In 1939, they joined others in founding the Old Town Club on 160 acres of Reynolda land. The construction of a new golf course provided work for many of Reynolda's laborers.

In the first seven years of their ownership, the Babcocks occupied Reynolda for vacations and holidays only. They and their four children—Katharine (known as Katie), Charles, Jr., Barbara, and Betsy—lived for most of the year in Greenwich, Connecticut. Charlie Babcock commuted from the affluent suburb to Manhattan and his job as a stockbroker. He and two partners—R. J.'s nephew Richard S. Reynolds, Jr., and Thomas Staley, a Reynolds family cousin—had founded Reynolds & Company in 1931.

While Charlie's career prospered, Mary devoted herself to redoing Reynolda. "In future, bungalow must keep present style," reads the heading on a page of notes in Mary's handwriting. Though undated, the list appears to be a summary prepared in advance of a consultation with an architect. The entries show that Mary wanted to modernize Reynolda without changing its character.

Included on her list was a new recreation center in the basement. It was to include a "modernistic" game room with a fireplace and a big window, a shooting gallery, a bowling alley, billiards and ping-pong tables, and an indoor pool. To these recreational features, all of which were built, were added a squash court and a wine vault, whose shelves were stocked by a Greenwich liquor store. (In 1980, a benefit auction of the remaining wine—651 bottles, including a Chateau Margaux 1928 that brought $550—raised $16,845 for Reynolda House, Museum of American Art.)

Mary's other requirements included more guest rooms and closets, a painting studio, and a flower room, the latter two presumably for herself, since she was a talented amateur painter and entered her floral arrangements in garden-club competitions. A modernized heating system and a laundry (the existing laundry was located in the village) were also on the list. She noted the need for a new entrance, too. Reynolda's existing main entrance, under the porte-cochere, brought visitors directly and unceremoniously into the reception hall, giving the family no privacy.

Charles Barton Keen would have been the logical architect to oversee the changes. But Keen had died in 1931, and his firm did not survive his

Charlie and Mary Babcock with Charles, Jr., Katharine, and Barbara, c. 1937

death. Mary hired the New York firm of Johnson & Porter as her architect and Eleanor Brown of the fashionable New York interior-design firm of McMillen & Company to refresh the interiors. Whatever expertise they contributed to the final effect, the actual changes made in the house and grounds conformed to Mary's original list.

Altogether, the alterations made little visible difference to the looks of Reynolda. As Mary had specified in her outline, the bungalow style was retained. The architects removed the old-fashioned porte-cochere, and a new sunken garden replaced the former forecourt. The new main entrance made use of an existing door in the east wing. The door was given more prominence by means of architectural ornamentation—an entablature above and pilasters at either side. The stair hall into which it opened was changed slightly in order to gain room for a proper vestibule with a powder room, coat closet, and telephone switchboard.

Some of the new recreational facilities were placed in former machine rooms and service areas in the basement. Space for the rest—including the new indoor pool and changing rooms and the squash court—was found in a formerly unexcavated section at ground level.

To accommodate more guests, a six-room guesthouse was built in the same style as the main house, with white plaster walls and a green tile roof. A breezeway connected the two structures.

Surviving blueprints and correspondence indicate that the improvements were started in 1936 and completed in 1938.

In 1935, on her twenty-eighth birthday, Mary gained direct control over her inheritance, which now totaled thirty million dollars. An article on the "Richest U.S. Women" in the November 1936 issue of *Fortune* stated that she was restoring "the huge family place in Winston-Salem, which is more like a community than an estate, to its former level of efficiency and [plans] to run it on a commercial basis." It sounded remarkably like something her mother might have said.

Mary also was her mother's daughter in matters of economy. She insisted to her decorator that the new guesthouse and existing children's playhouse be furnished economically. For Reynolda House, she authorized only repainting and reupholstering and new curtains, rugs, bedspreads, and lampshades. Another undated list, made in 1948 when the family relocated to Reynolda on a year-round basis, shows how furniture from its house in Greenwich was to be arranged at Reynolda.

The same meticulousness that Katharine had displayed was evident in a letter dated September 28, 1937, in which Mary issued instructions for bedroom-closet fittings with coordinated colors for shelf edging, hangers, luggage racks, and hat stands. For her own room, she speci-

Family reunion on June 21, 1941, showing former entrance
after porte-cochere and forecourt were removed and replaced by a sunken garden

fied blue and white satin hangers and hat stands, blue ensemble hangers, luggage racks painted blue with white tape, and, for the bath, a blue shower curtain.

Most of the interior improvements appear to have been completed by the fall of 1937. "Now that the house is all dressed up, I'd better get new uniforms for the staff," Mary wrote the housekeeper at Reynolda on October 16. "Please send sizes for Flora, Helen, Harvey and Albert. They will need new coats and possibly a dark suit, shirts & ties, better send shoe size of men just in case we do that, too."

Mary ran Reynolda from a distance, communicating on a first-name basis in letters with the resident housekeeper and secretary, Blanche Gunn. Besides items of local gossip, Gunn informed her employer when mail-order shipments

Guesthouse and indoor swimming pool, additions made by the Babcocks, c. 1937

REYNOLDA HOUSE ARCHIVES

Indoor swimming pool, with birdcages flanking fireplace, c. 1940

REYNOLDA HOUSE ARCHIVES

arrived from the New York stores. The deliveries included china, blankets, stationery, and three hundred pounds of white sand for the two twelve-and-a-half-foot-tall birdcages in the indoor swimming pool.

In advance of the family's arrivals, Gunn hired more staff and sometimes arranged matters for a party. For example, Mary once gave instructions for a gathering to take place at Reynolda following a dinner party at the Old Town Club. The party would return to Reynolda "for basement fun" about ten at night. "Have water put in pool, if possible. We will need a pin boy for bowling, maid at main door, and refreshments of popcorn, cheese and crackers, cigarettes (figure one pack per person) Coca Cola, Dr. Pepper, extra ice, and playing cards."

The Babcocks typically came to Reynolda for Thanksgiving, Christmas, and Easter. Some years, they also came during the summer as well. Sometimes, they traveled by rail, hiring a private Pullman car large enough to accommodate the family and some of the household staff. Rosalie Miller, the wife of Harvey Miller, Reynolda's butler, relished the experience of riding on the train and being served her meals by railroad

Harvey Miller, the Babcocks' butler

REYNOLDA HOUSE ARCHIVES

Harvey Miller decorating Christmas tree in reception hall

REYNOLDA HOUSE ARCHIVES

employees. Packing for the trip took two days, thanks to all the toys and clothes that the family wanted to bring down. In Winston-Salem, several trucks were sent to the railroad siding to pick up the luggage and transport it to the house, where the maids unpacked it.

It required twelve or more employees to run Reynolda when the family was in residence, Rosalie recalled when interviewed for an oral history in 1980. Among the staff were two bodyguards for the children. The bodyguards were engaged to guard against kidnapping, an omnipresent concern for wealthy families after the kidnapping and murder of the Lindbergh baby in 1932.

Working conditions at Reynolda House were at least as good as they had been in Katharine's day. Domestic employees received their salary even when out because of illness; when Flora Pledger, the cook, had to stay home for five weeks to care for her husband, who was dying of cancer, she was paid every week. Servants and their families also received medical attention, paid vacations, Christmas gifts from each of the Babcock children, and Christmas bonuses. A mark of respect especially appreciated by the staff was that they ate the same food the family did.

Flora, who worked for the Babcocks from 1935 until her retirement in 1962, remembered serving three meals a day at Reynolda to as many as thirty people, including servants. Menus were standard, except on special occasions when Mrs. Babcock would call her in for a conference. "Sunday dinner was always roast beef and vegetables, such as string beans, beets. Sunday-morning breakfast was sausage and apples," Flora reminisced. "They had soup every day for dinner, bean soup or vichyssoise, but you'd just go by the directions on the can."

When the family came to Reynolda, the house was filled with Winston-Salem relatives and friends, who were invited for big holiday parties and came for impromptu gatherings. The basement, with its large mural humorously caricaturing family and friends and its glamorous Art Deco bar with mirrored walls and red leather banquettes, was a popular destination for children as well as adults. "You could swim, roller-skate, bowl. We had parties all the time, and anybody was welcome," Katie Babcock Mountcastle recalled of her teenage years in the early 1950s.

There was an entrance into the game room directly from the lakeside, but "everyone entered through the front door, shook hands with Mother and Dad, chatted, and then went down to the basement," Barbara Babcock Millhouse reminisced.

The American entry into World War II in December 1941 brought changes to the Babcocks' way of life. Charlie volunteered for service in the

Mirrored Art Deco bar, with
Mary Babcock at left, c. 1937

REYNOLDA HOUSE ARCHIVES

Party in basement game room,
showing murals, c. 1950

REYNOLDA HOUSE ARCHIVES

Reception hall, c. 1917

REYNOLDA HOUSE ARCHIVES

Reception hall, c. 1980

REYNOLDA HOUSE ARCHIVES

United States Army, and Mary decided to bring the children to Winston-Salem for the war's duration. Katie recalled that the move took place with almost miraculous speed. "Pearl Harbor was December 7 and by Christmas we were at Reynolda," she said. The move, of course, may have been planned, since the family typically spent the holiday at Reynolda. But everyone who knew her well realized that Mary Babcock preferred Winston-Salem to Greenwich. Mary tried to interest her sister in joining her in Winston-Salem. "You could be very useful here, giving First Aid instruction," she wrote, but Nancy remained in Greenwich.

During the war, Mary and the children stayed in the cottage in Reynolda Village that once had been occupied by Reynolda's electrician, rather than at Reynolda House, which would have been difficult to run in a time of shortages and rationing.

Early in the war, there was a possibility that the big house would be used as a hospital or rehabilitation center for wounded GI's. The government never did take Reynolda House for this purpose, but the house was the setting for at least one party that Mary gave for military personnel stationed in and near Winston-Salem. At the party, a colonel played the organ and the rest of the soldiers roller-skated. Since gasoline was short, mules and hay wagons were used to transport guests to the house.

Mary planted a victory garden in the early spring of 1942 and canned and froze vegetables for home consumption. She devoted herself to raising the children, who were attending private school in Winston-Salem, and to writing almost daily letters to her husband. After receiving officer training, Charlie served in Europe as chief financial officer G-5 (for military-government and civil affairs) for American Headquarters, European Theater of Operations, attaining the rank of major. The record of Mary's war years in Winston-Salem survives in her letters, which Charlie saved.

There were still servants to cook meals and do housekeeping chores during this period. But the life revealed in her letters was a relatively simple one, centered around the children's developing personalities, as shown by their schoolwork and small adventures. Mary worked as a nurse's aide in a hospital, as a canteen worker for the American Red Cross, and as a driver for a motor-corps unit. She also taught arts and crafts in a public school in northern Winston-Salem. Gas was rationed and travel by train was crowded, but the family went up to Roaring Gap in the summer, and Mary and Charlie were occasionally able to spend time together before he was sent overseas.

In peacetime, she had relied on Charlie to tend to many of the financial details of overseeing Reynolda, but Mary now was doing it herself, occasionally writing of the difficulties of running the place and asking his advice on various matters.

Charlie and Mary Babcock during World War II, c. 1944
Photograph courtesy of Barbara Babcock Millhouse

Charles H. Babcock, 1899–1967

Babcock children in pony carts at Reynolda, c. 1939
Photograph courtesy of Barbara Babcock Millhouse

As the war wound down, she worried over the future of Reynolda House. "From all we read & see we all know that the day of big estates is passing," she wrote Nancy on February 6, 1945. "I'm planning to sell off the church side of the road right after the war in pieces, selling as much as the town can absorb. Property around the Old Town Club will be sold after that, probably 10 or 20 years later. But the big house & gardens etc. are what cause upkeep expense." As for the house, she wrote, "We've always felt that it would have to go to a university, orphanage or something before I was old enough to die. But they aren't as interested in accepting estates as they once were."

Winston-Salem had grown out to include Reynolda, which in 1940 was placed within the city limits. "City taxes will be heavy," Mary added in her letter to Nancy. "Tom Butler [a financial adviser and head of the Safe Deposit and Trust Company] worries about the investment necessary to support the place. I feel that perhaps it would be better to sell the place instead of having it torn down for tax reasons someday. . . . I hate to let it go while the children are reaching an age when they enjoy its facilities. . . . I've really become attached to it, but not so attached that I'd want to be a pauper to keep it."

In 1945, a representative of the chamber of commerce suggested that five hundred acres of Reynolda's land be used for a hospital, Mary confided in a letter to Nancy. "Last night I was approached on whether I would sell. . . . I believe if they'll take it, it'll be our only chance for many years to come. How do you feel on the subject? I have written my business advisors . . . to ask about the effect of such an institution on surrounding property, especially since it's a psychiatric type of institution. . . . I can see where it might be the nicest way to keep it intact and yet if mishandled it could be a horrible outcome."

The idea was quickly abandoned. "Everyone I asked (business advisors) blew up over Reynolda becoming a vet's hospital," she wrote Nancy on February 16, 1945. "One said I'd ruin Winston-Salem, especially its remaining residential property, and so would not have a friend in this town. . . . So I guess Reynolda will go on as is to live a longer life and end as an ancient ruin, but with the charm of its homey atmosphere still there."

In July 1946, a little more than a year after Mary had wondered whether a hospital would be a good idea, she and her husband found another use for 350 acres of Reynolda's land. They offered it to Wake Forest College if the small Baptist institu-tion, founded in 1834 and located about a hundred miles away, near Raleigh, would agree to move to Winston-Salem.

Helped along by generous funding by the Bowman Gray family, Wake Forest's medical school already had moved to the city in 1941, after becoming affiliated with the Baptist hospital there. The idea of bringing the rest of the school was shared by a number of people at the college and in Winston-Salem, including Will Reynolds, who issued a formal invitation to the school on February 27, 1946. Besides the promise that the college would not be asked to change its name, the major inducement he offered was a grant "in perpetuity" of $350,000 a year from the Z. Smith Reynolds Foundation. Later, a donation of $2 million for new buildings was announced if the school agreed to move. The anonymous donor was Will Reynolds.

For Wake Forest, relocating could revitalize a school outgrowing its present quarters and in need of the financial support available in a wealthy city. For Winston-Salem, the school would round out the city's higher-education facilities. Salem College (for women) and Winston-Salem State College (solely for blacks at that time) had excellent reputations. But there was no college that would admit white men, a lack that Will Reynolds and other leaders in Winston-Salem felt should be remedied.

The Babcocks' offer of land was read aloud on July 30 at a special Baptist State Convention in Winston-Salem convened to consider the question of relocating the school. Besides "at least three hundred acres [which] an outstanding college planning authority has determined . . . to be a most desirably located area for a college campus," the Babcocks' letter promised additional land to help the college grow.

After listening to the contents of the letter, an estimated 95 percent of the 2,245 delegates gave approval to the move by voice vote. The legal right of the Z. Smith Reynolds Foundation to commit part of its income in perpetuity was ratified by the North Carolina Supreme Court on June 5, 1947, and plans for the move then began in earnest.

On October 15, 1951, President Harry S. Truman visited Winston-Salem to break ground for Wake Forest's new campus. He used the occasion to make a speech on foreign policy. The content of the speech is not remembered locally. But many people know that Truman took a presidential nap on the sofa in R. J.'s former den in the east wing of Reynolda House after a luncheon of roast turkey and baked ham. Truman's trip is also recalled as the sixth official visit to North Carolina by an American president.

The Babcocks more than kept their promise to Wake Forest. After Mary Babcock died of cancer in 1953, the Mary Reynolds Babcock Foundation was created by her will. The foundation, run by Charlie Babcock, continued to provide generous gifts of land and money to the college and to many other worthy institutions and causes.

In the early 1950s, Five Row was replaced by a portion of Silas Creek Parkway. In 1957, the old polo field became the site of a public school. A few years later, the private Summit School acquired adjacent Reynolda land through donation by the Babcocks and purchase. But approximately 605 acres of Reynolda land—more than half the original 1,067 acres—now belong to Wake Forest. The main campus, the football stadium, and an attractive neighborhood of private homes occupied by faculty and school administrators are all on former Reynolda acreage. Charlie Babcock also gave Reynolda Gardens, Reynolda Village, and an income-producing tract with a large industrial building on it to Wake Forest.

Outwardly the same as ever, the old farm buildings in the village have produced hundreds of thousands of dollars of rental income for the Wake Forest operating budget. "Charlie Babcock wanted the village to have life—activities and people, but no commercialization. . . . He never considered a major grocery store or a chain store," recalled Bill Bondurant, a former director of the Mary Reynolds Babcock Foundation.

Beginning in 1978, in a relatively early example

President Truman breaks ground on the Reynolda site that was to become the campus of Wake Forest College, October 15, 1951. From left to right are Charlie Babcock, Truman, Judge Hubert Olive, Odis Mull, and Harold W. Tribble, the president of the college.

of the now-common practice of adaptive reuse, the university developed the village so that exterior changes were kept to a minimum. Under the direction of local architect Edwin Bouldin, the project refitted the interiors of old cow barns, corncribs, and cottages to serve as small shops, offices, and restaurants. Concessions to commerce included parking lots and paved walkways and roads, but a rural feeling was preserved.

By the late 1950s, it had become clear that Reynolda House would not be a family home for the Babcocks very much longer. In 1954, Charlie Babcock married Winifred Penn Knies, who had family ties in southern California. By 1960, they were spending summers in California and had contracted to build a new house on a beautiful piece of property a few miles west of Reynolda. The house, called Westerly, was near Bethabara, the site of the original Moravian settlement in North Carolina, which was undergoing excavation with Charlie's help.

In 1963, Babcock agreed to allow Piedmont University Center to use Reynolda House as its headquarters. The center was an experimental cooperative of seventeen (later twenty-one) liberal-arts colleges in North Carolina. Though formed earlier, the center became increasingly active in the 1960s. A new executive director, A. R. Keppel, launched a vigorous program that brought eminent speakers to North Carolina for joint programs and academic conferences, sponsored cultural events, and engaged in cooperative buying and other activities.

As was typical of Charlie Babcock's common-sense arrangements, Keppel and his wife moved into the house in December 1964, giving Reynolda House responsible caretakers while its use as a center for nonprofit activities took it off the tax rolls. Meanwhile, Piedmont University Center received a management fee for the Keppels' caretaking duties, which helped defray the costs of operation. It was, however, a temporary arrangement which either party could cancel with notice. The center shared Reynolda House for eleven years, moving out in 1975. During this period, a new destiny was worked out for Reynolda House as a museum of American art.

Chapter 7

REYNOLDA HOUSE AS A MUSEUM

Reynolda House might have been altered beyond recognition or even abandoned when Piedmont University Center lost momentum toward the end of the 1960s. But extremes were not necessary because a new use was found for the house as a center for the arts. This course preserved Reynolda's character for a new generation to enjoy.

Charlie Babcock, who died in December 1967 shortly after the formal opening of Reynolda House, had envisioned his former home in a new role as early as 1964, if not before. His intention was spelled out in the charter of Reynolda House, Inc., which was adopted at the first board meeting in Winston-Salem, on December 18, 1964.

Reynolda House would add "Museum of American Art" to its official name later. In addition to Babcock and his daughter Barbara Millhouse (then Lassiter), who was elected president, the board included Betsy Babcock (Charlie's youngest daughter), Nancy Reynolds, Anne Reynolds Forsyth (the daughter of Smith Reynolds and Anne Cannon), Dale Gramley (president of Salem College), A. R. Keppel, and Leon I. Rice, Jr. (a local attorney).

After accepting the gift of the house and its 19.1-acre site from the Mary Reynolds Babcock Foundation, the board made one of its first actions the adoption of a charter stating in part that Reynolda House would be a "center for the encouragement and advancement of the arts and higher education" and "a public museum" with a "display of fine paintings, sculpture, rare books, art objects and furniture and furnishings."

By preserving their former home as a historic house museum and an educational institution for the arts, the Babcocks were participating in a growing national movement to save American buildings of historic interest from destruction. Charlie Babcock had informed the National Trust for Historic Preservation about his plans for Reynolda and in 1964 had received a letter commending them. He also was well aware of two American historic preservations that set new standards: Colonial Williamsburg in Williamsburg, Virginia, and the Winterthur Museum of American Art in Wilmington, Delaware. In the 1950s, as an active participant in a successful effort to save the old Moravian section in Winston-Salem now known as Old Salem, he had been part of a group that intensively studied the example of Colonial Williamsburg. Charlie and his new wife entertained Henry Francis DuPont and his wife at Reynolda on April 10, 1961. Later that year, the Babcocks were invited by DuPont to visit him at his home, Winterthur, which he had converted into a museum of American decorative arts.

An arts center at Reynolda House also fit into a statewide pattern of interest in the visual arts that began to grow in the 1950s and reached a crescendo in the mid-1960s. This development led to the formation or expansion of museums, art galleries, arts councils, and art schools all over North Carolina. In 1956, for example, the state legislature provided the North Carolina Museum of Art with its own building in Raleigh. The same year in Winston-Salem, the Gallery of Fine Arts, devoted to the work of regional artists, opened; it survives as the Southeastern Center for Contemporary Art, or SECCA, now quartered in the former home of James G. Hanes half a mile from Reynolda. In 1958, the Ackland Art Museum opened at the University of North Carolina. In 1963, under Governor Terry Sanford, the state established a summer program in Winston-Salem for artistically gifted students, which later became the North Carolina School of the Arts. The North Carolina Arts Council was born on December 3, 1964, as a temporary body under the chairmanship of R. Philip Hanes, Jr., of Winston-Salem. It became permanent in April 1966. The Museum of Early Southern Decorative Arts opened in Old Salem in 1965. The same year, a committee of North Carolinians was restoring the Governor's Mansion in Raleigh.

As one of the area's first families, the Babcocks were involved in the regional interest in the arts. Barbara Millhouse recalled that in the 1950s, her father was asked to donate a painting to the North

Carolina Museum of Art. Around the same time, her father and stepmother began to take a great interest in painting. "Winifred had an art epiphany inspired by a painting by Franz Kline, and my father called me on the telephone one day and told me to rush down to a gallery to see some paintings by Ernst Ludwig Kirchner [a German Expressionist] that he was planning to buy," said Barbara.

If other communities in North Carolina were organizing museums and restoring significant buildings, Winston-Salem could do no less. "The idea of being first in some activity related to the arts is seemingly irresistible to Winston," wrote Alvin Toffler in "Winston-Salem, Culturopolis of the South," an article in the March 1964 issue of *Show: The Magazine of the Arts*. Toffler, now known as a trend spotter and author of *Future Shock* and *The Third Wave*, noted that "Winston has no art museum as such and even its most vociferous culture boosters confess that there are no private collections of first-rate importance."

This was the kind of statement guaranteed to goad Winston-Salem's culture lovers to action. Two temporary displays of fine art showed that the city had an appetite for the visual arts. During the Christmas season of 1963, Thalhimer's department store put on a two-week exhibition of artworks by regional painters, using its store windows and second floor as a "gallery." Around the same time, a temporary exhibition of eighty-eight works of art by masters such as Van Dyck, Rubens, Tiepolo, Corot, and Picasso took place at the Forsyth County Library, which occupied the site of the old Fifth Street house to which R. J. Reynolds had brought his bride in 1905. The paintings, exhibited by New York dealers, were said to be worth over $1.5 million, and $250,000 worth of art was sold.

On September 15, 1965, Reynolda House began opening its doors to the public two afternoons a week. "People lined up to come here," said Barbara Millhouse, who is still president as of this writing. "But the question was always, How are we going to create a cultural experience so meaningful that people will stop looking at the house as simply an instance of how rich people lived?" One answer was to exhibit noteworthy works of art. The first special exhibition in 1965 consisted of paintings collected by members of the Reynolds family. The following year, a display of jewelry designed by Salvador Dali was so popular that the show was extended for a week. Also in 1966, as part of the celebration of the city's bicentennial, Reynolda House mounted a "picture a month" series. The idea, suggested by Ruth Julian, a local collector, was to put on display each month a borrowed work of art related to America's heritage, such as Gilbert Stuart's portrait of George Washington.

Barbara Babcock Lassiter (Millhouse) with Mrs. M. C. Benton, the mayor's wife,
opening Reynolda House to the public on September 15, 1965

Meanwhile, Reynolda's board was planning to acquire a permanent art collection. The Art Acquisitions Fund had been established with a hundred thousand dollars each from the Mary Reynolds Babcock Foundation and the Z. Smith Reynolds Foundation and a hundred thousand dollars from other sources, including Anne Reynolds Forsyth and the Arca Foundation, established by Nancy Reynolds.

While Barbara Millhouse mulled over what kind of artworks to acquire, the April "picture of the month" was John Singleton Copley's *Portrait of Winslow Warren*, on loan from the Boston Museum of Fine Arts. Stuart Feld, a curator in the department of American painting and sculpture at the Metropolitan Museum of Art in New York, came to Winston-Salem to lecture on the painting on April 21, 1966. After dinner in the Reynolda House dining room, Barbara asked Feld's advice. He suggested focusing on American

Students writing on Frederic E. Church's *The Andes of Ecuador*

paintings, especially those of the nineteenth century, which currently were not in critical favor. "We could not raise more than three hundred thousand dollars, which at the time would have purchased only an indifferent canvas by Monet," recalled Barbara. "American art was an area in which we could build a good collection." She not only took Feld's advice, but secured his guidance as an informal adviser. Feld drew up a list of artists to consider and encouraged her to purchase a now-celebrated painting, *The Andes of Ecuador* (1855) by Frederic E. Church.

With the first acquisitions in 1966–67, Reynolda's leaders made several important decisions which have continued to guide the museum's art purchases. Works by Americans would be chosen, and each would be the best-available example of that artist's output. The collection would be limited in size to the hanging space in the house. During 1966 and 1967, the acquisitions committee bought nine paintings by American artists. Among them were *The Andes of Ecuador, Sierra Nevada* (c. 1871–73) by Albert Bierstadt, *Mrs. Harrison Gray Otis* (1809) by Gilbert Stuart, *Job Lot Cheap* (1878) by William M. Harnett, and *In the Studio* (1884) by William Merritt Chase.

These works, now considered splendid examples of American painting, can be seen hanging at Reynolda House along with other noteworthy canvases. After Feld helped chart the course, Barbara set out on her own to research the field of American painting. She focused her collecting in this area and also encouraged family members to make purchases of American art for the museum. Two of the first paintings to be added to those purchased with the original funds were John Singleton Copley's *John Spooner* (1763), a gift from Nancy Reynolds, and Thomas Eakins's *A. W. Lee* (1905), a gift from Nancy Reynolds and Barbara Millhouse. Charles Willson Peale's *Mr. and Mrs. Alexander Robinson* (1795), Thomas Sully's *Jared Sparks* (1831), Thomas Cole's *Home in the Woods* (1847), William Sidney Mount's *The Card Players* (c. 1847–50), Maurice Prendergast's *The Bathing Cove* (c. 1916–18), Georgia O'Keeffe's *Pool in the Woods* (1922), Thomas Hart Benton's *Bootleggers* (1927), and Grant Wood's *Spring Turning* (1936) were all gifts from Barbara Millhouse. Mary Babcock's youngest daughter, Betsy, contributed Joseph Stella's *Tree, Cactus, Moon* (c. 1928), Audrey Flack's *Bounty* (1978), and a sculpture by Alexander Calder.

Individuals unrelated to the family also have donated artworks. Collector R. Philip Hanes, Jr., donated *Natural Bridge, Va.* (1860), by David Johnson. Art dealer Lee Ault offered Horace Pippin's *The Whipping* (1941), and Maynard Weber and his wife gave *The Dancers* (1948), painted by his father, Max Weber. The Webers made the

Visitors discussing *Bootleggers* by Thomas Hart Benton

donation after a casual visit to Reynolda House, during which they were impressed by the enthusiastic discussion of artworks among groups of young people.

Reynolda's first acquisitions were made at a strategic time. In a few years, critics began to look far more favorably on American art, and Reynolda's paintings began to rise in critical esteem and value. The collection received national exposure in 1971 when the paintings were exhibited in New York at the Hirschl & Adler Gallery (where Stuart Feld was now one of the partners) in a benefit showing for Barbara Millhouse's alma mater, Smith College. An article in *Antiques* magazine made the collection public knowledge among an audience that counted.

Over the years, purchases and gifts expanded the art collection greatly. By the fall of 1996, it included 158 paintings, sculptures, works on paper, fine-art ceramics, and photographs. The print collection was started in 1976 with the purchase of twenty-four works by major 1970s artists and six etchings by John Sloan.

Having embarked on the museum path, Reynolda's board soon realized that it took more than fine paintings to attract an audience. It took programs. In 1970, the board appointed the first full-time director of Reynolda House to design and carry them out. He was Nicholas Burton Bragg, an alumnus of Wake Forest who had done graduate work in history at the University of North Carolina at Chapel Hill. After four years at the North Carolina Department of Archives and History in Raleigh, he came to Reynolda House from Old Salem, where he had served as director of education and interpretation.

Bragg, who celebrated his twenty-sixth year at Reynolda in 1996, developed a series of unique programs with the Reynolda art collection as the focus. A four-week summer program in American creativity known as "American Foundations" was the prototype and continues today. Intended for college students and postgraduates and given jointly with Wake Forest University, it broke new ground in interdisciplinary education. The faculty included an art historian and professors of music and American literature. In addition to listening to faculty lectures, each student selected one of the artworks on display at Reynolda to study in depth and relate to the same period's music and literature.

Bragg found ways to apply the American Foundations approach to programs of shorter duration for other groups—museum docents, seniors, schoolchildren, and even youthful offenders and unwed, pregnant teenage girls. He also instituted a lively array of literary and musical programs, including late-night events for night owls.

Reynolda House started with the idea that the

Director Nicholas Bragg, assistant director of development Elizabeth Morgan,
and board member Leslie M. Baker in front of Thomas Cole's *Home in the Woods*

American Foundations, a summer graduate program, in session in the enclosed lake porch, c. 1992

rooms of the house would be a backdrop to art and programs. Some visitors did not necessarily agree. Many were—and are—attracted to the house because of its history. They wanted to know about the furniture and other objects that belonged to the Reynolds and Babcock families, and about the people who built Reynolda and lived in it.

Today, the museum offers fine arts, educational programs, and a look at the history of Reynolda House as a family home. Nancy Reynolds initiated this effort in 1973 when she funded the restoration and exhibition of clothing belonging to her mother and other members of the family, stored over the years in the attic. Redesigned as an exhibition hall, the attic now houses a lively collection of clothing, toys, decorative objects, and personal artifacts owned by members of the Reynolds and Babcock families. These colorful objects, dating from 1895 to 1962, range from

Nancy Reynolds and Pete Ballard discussing the costume collection, 1973

wedding dresses worn by Katharine, Mary, and Nancy to R. J.'s cigar cutter. Among the items of apparel that have been placed on view are the beribboned negligee Katharine made for her trousseau, her Marie Antoinette masquerade costume, a suit worn by R. J., Dick's naval uniform, and other heirlooms. Adding a further note of the past, the Aeolian organ is played regularly on Sunday afternoons.

More than one million guests have come to Reynolda since its inception as a museum, over half of them to attend one of the numerous programs. In 1996, there were special events on 206 of the 310 days the museum was open.

No building can withstand extensive use without occasional refurbishing. Reynolda House has been refurbished several times, notably in 1991 and 1992, when it was closed for more than a year to install environmental controls and put in place other improvements. The new systems turned Reynolda House from an old family home serving as a museum into a museum in an old family home. The difference may be subtle, but it is understood by every museum official. By putting in these environmental controls, the board brought Reynolda House into line with the latest museum practices. Among other advantages, the improvements let Reynolda borrow artworks from other museums.

In order to fund the improvements, Reynolda House went beyond family funding and launched a public capital campaign in 1990 with a goal of $5.2 million. By 1992, $6.2 million was raised. Besides $3.25 million from family foundations and Barbara Millhouse, there were grants from the Kresge Foundation and the National Endowment for the Arts, as well as more than $1 million from Winston-Salem corporations such as the R. J. Reynolds Tobacco Company, Sara Lee, and Wachovia Bank.

During the renovations, a nineteen-month national tour of forty paintings took place. Under the auspices of the American Federation of Arts, "American Originals: Selections from Reynolda House, Museum of American Art" toured museums in seven cities around the country. The exhibition catalog, published by Abbeville Press in 1990, further extended knowledge of the Reynolda House collection.

American Federation of Arts director Myrna Smoot explained the organization's sponsorship of the exhibition: "There is no shortage in this country of museums with respectable collections of American art. Only a handful, however, have collections as thoroughly first rate as that of Reynolda House." She went on to call the collection "an illuminating chronicle of the key developments in American art."

Only a small minority of the thousands of museums in the United States choose to undergo the rigorous professional accreditation examination of the American Association of Museums. In 1996, some 744 museums had such certification, including 24 in North Carolina.

Since Reynolda House's goals were different from the norm, its leaders knew the museum would not necessarily receive accreditation when they first applied in 1972. But the visiting experts were impressed enough to approve the application. "It is one of the most exciting educational experiments using original art as its basis we have seen," said the accreditation report of June 14, 1972.

In 1982, the museum was reexamined. "Reynolda House continues to be unconventional, and to a large degree this is the reason for its success. Reynolda is not simply an art museum. . . . It is . . . a multi-disciplinary educational center which seeks through its art collection, music and literary resources to

Barbara Millhouse taking Lady Bird Johnson and her secretary on a tour of the art collection, April 22, 1983

Director Nicholas Bragg with docents

explore the cultural milieu of the American past."

A third certification report in 1996 found that "Reynolda House is unique among American museums . . . a collection which is in its first generation, one in which the role of the collector is part of today's experience. At the same time, the special nature of the educational experience makes it one of the most intellectually stimulating places to visit. There is time here to discuss and learn."

Reynolda's strengths, as summarized by the American Association of Museums' accreditation committee in July 1996, included its art collection, which reflects all the major periods of American art; its building, a fine example of an American country house; the interesting family artifacts displayed throughout the house; and its public programs "for all ages [and in] all kinds of formats."

The truest tests for any museum are whether it can attract a wide audience and broad-based support. Reynolda, though a young museum, has met those tests.

The history of Reynolda House can be divided into three periods: a golden age under Katharine Reynolds Johnston, a renaissance under Mary Reynolds Babcock, and development as a public institution under the leadership of Barbara Millhouse. What next?

"All institutions must grow and change," said Barbara. "But I am certain that using the collection and the setting for education in the arts will remain the basic mission of Reynolda House."

INDEX